Shakespeare *for* Kids

HIS LIFE AND TIMES

(21) ACTIVITIES

COLLEEN AAGESEN AND MARGIE BLUMBERG

CHICAGO
REVIEW
PRESS

Library of Congress Cataloging-in-Publication Data

Aagesen, Colleen.

Shakespeare for kids : his life and times : 21 activities / Colleen Aagesen & Margie Blumberg.

p.   cm.

Summary: Presents the life and works of Shakespeare. Includes activities to introduce Elizabethan times, including making costumes, making and using a quill pen, and binding a book by hand.

ISBN 1-55652-347-5

1. Shakespeare, William, 1564–1616—Juvenile literature. 2. Dramatists, English—Early modern, 1500–1700—Biography—Juvenile literature. 3. England—Social life and customs—16th century—Juvenile literature. [1. Shakespeare, William, 1564–1616. 2. Authors, English. 3. England—Social life and customs—16th century. 4. Handicraft.] I. Blumberg, Margie. II. Title.

PR2895.A24 1999	98-49686
822.3'3—dc21	CIP
[b]	AC

Interior design by Mel Kupfer

Front Cover Art: Fencers, *Paradoxes of Defence*, George Silver (1599), courtesy of the British Library, Department of Printed Books. *View of London*, courtesy of the Library of Congress. Eighteenth-century water-color of The Globe, courtesy of the British Museum. Droushout portrait, *First Folio*, courtesy of the Records Office, Shakespeare Birthplace Trust, Stratford-Upon-Avon. Back Cover Art: London Bridge, detail from *View of London*; reconstruction drawing of The Globe stage; and Shakespeare and contemporaries, courtesy of the Library of Congress.

Published by Chicago Review Press, Incorporated
814 North Franklin Street
Chicago, Illinois 60610
ISBN-13: 978-1-55652-347-2
ISBN-10: 1-55652-347-5
Printed in Singapore by CS Graphics

COLLEEN AAGESEN

To my parents, Royce and Charlotte Jean Harper—
The hand that had made you fair hath made you good.

MARGIE BLUMBERG

For my dear family and friends, with love—
For you in my respect are all the world.

contents

SHAK SPEARE

From an original Picture in the Possession of the late Duke of Chandois.

Prologue

The Stone Bridge Is Still There. The house that William Shakespeare called home and the school and the church that he attended still stand in the same place they stood in the quaint market town of Stratford-upon-Avon in 1564. If William could return with you to his hometown, he would surely take you to the market where his father and other tradespeople sold their goods each Thursday. He would lead you to the inn yards where traveling players performed. He might even show you the grammar school where the teachers drilled language into the minds of their young pupils—and where the beauty of words found a place in the heart and soul of one schoolboy in particular.

When their first son, William, was born in 1564, John and Mary Arden Shakespeare could not have dreamed how spectacular his future would be. Their son would perform for Queen Elizabeth I. His name would be forever linked to hers.

By 1564, Elizabeth I, the 31-year-old daughter and only child of King Henry VIII and Anne Boleyn, had been England's queen for six years. As with many countries throughout history, Elizabeth's England had its shining moments and its disappointments. The land was a mixture of rich and poor, good health and disease, bountiful harvests and famines. And although England was at peace within its own borders, the queen was forever sending her men out to fight battles in foreign lands. To escape a bit from their struggles, the English people found pleasure in recreation.

William Shakespeare was born into a country that enjoyed its games, sports, and holiday fairs. Fortunately, Elizabeth herself loved a good show. Her blessings on entertainment, great and small, endeared the queen to her subjects and set the stage for Shakespeare's genius. When Shakespeare moved to the city, theater was alive in the London landscape. For 20 years, William Shakespeare gave the English wonderful theater, becoming a famous and wealthy man. His plays captured the hearts of the English people, as he spoke to their deepest feelings and passions. And he did it all with amazing style and wit.

Still, Shakespeare's plays might have vanished on closing nights were it not for a man in another time and place—a German inventor named Johannes Gutenberg who in the mid 1400s gave the world movable metal type. Within eighteen years, the first book was published.

The year William Shakespeare was born, the Italian artist Michelangelo died. By 1564, Michelangelo's statue *David* had been on majestic footing for 60 years, and Leonardo da Vinci's masterpiece, the *Mona Lisa*, had been smiling mysteriously for 61 years. Yes, the Renaissance had flowered in Italy, but England was still waiting for Shakespeare.

By the year of Shakespeare's birth, ocean adventurers had pushed back the globe's physical boundaries. Columbus found the Bahamas in 1492 and, nine years later, Amerigo Vespucci explored the coast of South America. Vasco Nuñez de Balboa reached the Pacific Ocean in 1513 and, nine years after that, Ferdinand Magellan's sailors returned to Spain, the first to sail around the earth. Scholars, who had been looking to the stars for centuries, reached a new dawn when, in 1543, a Polish monk, Nicolaus Copernicus, correctly claimed that the Sun—not the Earth—was the center of the solar system.

Into this age of adventure and promise, an imaginative child with perfect timing was born. As if on cue, the printing presses were running and Queen Elizabeth was ready to be amused. The stars were in alignment for a fireworks of drama the world has been enjoying ever since.

THE early years
A WORLD FULL of WONDERS

April 1564 through 1577. In Stratford-upon-Avon, Warwickshire, England, William Shakespeare is born, sees his first play, and attends school.

All the world's a stage . . .
And one man in his time plays many parts . . .
At first, the infant . . .

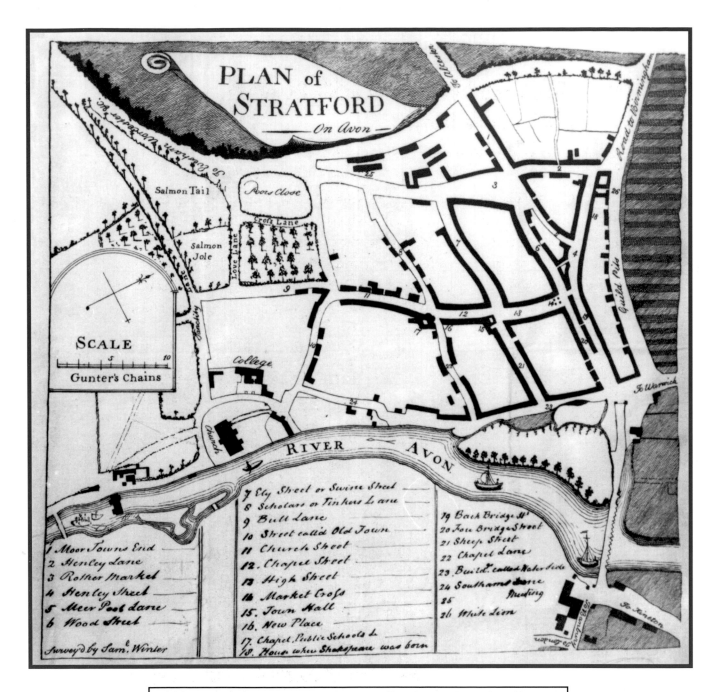

The earliest known map of Stratford-upon-Avon

act 1, scene 1 John and Mary Arden Shakespeare welcome a baby.

A Springtime Gift. John and Mary Shakespeare's new arrival, a good-natured, rosy-cheeked boy named William, had been softly cooing all morning. As Mary tenderly lifted her son from his rocking crib, she adjusted his cap and straightened a painted linen cloth hanging on the living room wall. Stepping outside with him into the warm sun of the *middle summer's spring* (the debut of midsummer), she felt joyous holding a baby tightly in her arms again. A few years earlier, she had lost her first two children, Joan and Margaret, when they were only infants. Their lives had been as fleeting as a violet's . . . *sweet, not lasting, the perfume . . . of a minute—no more.* Now, with William, she felt happy to be a mother once again.

On the Street Where He Lived. John and Mary Shakespeare were undoubtedly proud and happy as they introduced their new baby to their friends on Henley Street. Although we don't know how many neighbors and relatives came to share in their joy that spring, today, more than 400 years later, 2 million people visit Stratford-upon-Avon each year.

Alas. The date of William Shakespeare's birth was not recorded. However, his baptism at Holy Trinity Church on Wednesday, April 26, 1564, was registered. Because the church required that the ceremony be held within a few days of birth, historians have assigned April 23rd as his birth date. Assuming this date is true, and because he died on April 23, 1616, his life span was exactly 52 years.

Henley Street is the street on which the Shakespeare family lived.

Solid Ground

The layout of William Shakespeare's hometown of 109 acres has not changed since its founding in 1196!

Definitions

What's in a name? The name of the town, Stratford-upon-Avon, comes from the following words:

The Old English word for *ancient road* is *straet*.

Ford means a shallow place in a stream or river where one can cross.

Avon is from the Welsh word *afon* meaning river.

Half-Timber

The construction of the Shakespeare home is called "half-timbered." The oak framing of the house was constructed by attaching vertical posts to horizontal posts with flexible twigs and tree branches. To finish the walls—the other "half" of this half-timbered house—these twigs and tree branches were then plastered with clay and straw.

At Home

The Shakespeares's two charming houses stood among the ash, willow, poplar, oak, lime, and almost a thousand elm trees that graced this ancient river town. One building was used as the family's living quarters and the other was John Shakespeare's workshop.

Wishing Upon a Star. If John and Mary were like most Elizabethans, they believed that a person's personality and health were influenced by the combination of each of the four *humours* (basic fluids) in the body: blood, phlegm, choler, and black bile. As they admired their new baby, they had to wonder how these fluids would blend in him: Would William have too much blood (and be exceedingly hopeful and confident); phlegm (and be too apathetic and slow); choler (and be mostly irritable and angry); or black bile (and be predominantly sad and depressed)? Or would he have a harmonious mixture of these four fluids and be even-tempered and healthy?

And what about the stars? Many people thought that the position of the stars and the planets on a baby's day of birth determined the proportion of the humours in the body. Thus, they believed, a person's destiny was decided by the stars and planets on the day he was born.

What were Mary and John Shakespeare wishing for? *Belike* (probably) just a healthy, happy child. Stargazers would later say that William had been born under the influence of a *rhyming planet.*

William Shakespeare's Birthplace

My Life, My Joy, My Food, My All the World. A child was everything to an Elizabethan parent. But creating a family was difficult and so often disheartening in the 16th century. Fires, natural disasters, and diseases such as the influenza (flu) and the measles sadly took many lives. And the threat of bubonic plague epidemics, which had been periodically invading England since 1348, kept them ever vigilant.

The Elizabethans didn't know what caused the bubonic plague, but with each new outbreak, they followed the advice of authorities who had been observing the disease throughout the years. For instance, families that were affected by the plague stayed inside their homes throughout the illness. They kept their doors and windows shut and cleaned or destroyed sheets, blankets, pillows, and clothes.

Many Elizabethans believed that the plague was caused by *foule stinkyng aire* (bad-smelling air). They thought that if they replaced this bad air with sweet-scented air, they would be protected. So, they sat among the fruit trees, carried pomander balls, and kept rosemary near their noses and mouths.

Holy Trinity Church

Act 1 / 5

Definitions

Elizabethans were the people of England who lived during the reign of Queen Elizabeth I, from 1558 to 1603.

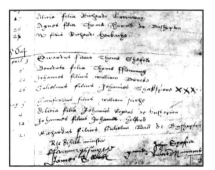

William Shakespeare's baptismal record reads in Latin: *Gulielmus* (William) *filius* (son of) *Johannes* (John) *Shakspere* (Shakespeare).

Today, we know how the plague spread: Rats were allowed to accumulate in the cities and country towns. The garbage in the cities and towns and the thatched roofs where rats burrowed were breeding grounds for them and their fleas. This was a danger- ous situation because rats are susceptible to a certain bacteria called *Yersinia pestis*. *Yersinia pestis* eventual- ly killed the rats and caused the plague in people. Before the rats died from the bacteria, the fleas bit the rats and became infected. And when the fleas ran

The living room of William Shakespeare's Henley Street home

out of rats to bite, they bit people. The infection that resulted caused many symptoms such as severe pain in the back and legs, headaches, a high pulse rate, high fever (102° F and above), and a feeling of apathy or delirium. The patient usually died within two days to one month after the sickness began. Other forms of the plague—one was transmitted by breathing drops of infected air from another person—caused different symptoms. But the result was the same—death.

The year before William was born, 80,000 people died from the plague in London. And the year of William's birth, 254 of his 1,500–2,000 neighbors perished when the Earl of Warwick's army brought the disease back with them from France. William's mother, Mary, may have believed it was because of her use of sweet-smelling pomander balls and herbs—and perhaps she even tucked a sprig of rosemary behind her baby's ear as he slept—that her newborn was shielded from this often fatal disease.

A Pomander Ball

Herb or Spice?

What is the difference between an herb and a spice?

Herbs such as basil, thyme, and mint come from leaves of plants that grow in regions of the world with temperate climates (neither too hot nor too cold). England has a temperate climate. Spices—vegetable substances such as cinnamon, pepper, and nutmeg—grow in tropical climates. India, one of the oldest civilizations in the world, has a tropical climate.

 s you will soon discover, pomander balls have a strong aroma. Because of this, they were used by the Elizabethans and generations of people before them to ward off the plague and other diseases that they believed were caused by bad-smelling air. It was a traditional practice for people to carry these aromatic balls in their hands, in boxes, or in pockets for protection. Or people could attach them to chains and wear them around their necks or waists. Today, we know that diseases are not caused by smelly air. Nevertheless, we can still enjoy the pomander ball's sweet aroma!

Materials

❊ Thick-skinned orange (you may also use a lemon, grapefruit, or lime)
❊ Fork
❊ 1 box of whole cloves
❊ Bowl
❊ Allspice, pumpkin pie spice, or 1 tablespoon each of cinnamon, nutmeg, and ginger
❊ Ribbons, lace, or netting

Choose a thick-skinned fruit. Because it is difficult to attach a clove to a fruit with broken skin, make sure the fruit is free of tears.

With a fork, randomly poke holes into the orange. The holes should not be so deep that the cloves fall in—you want the cloves to show!

Fill the holes with cloves.

Put the orange into a bowl and sprinkle the spices (allspice or pumpkin pie spice or a combination of cinnamon, nutmeg, and ginger) over the orange.

Keep the pomander ball in the bowl and let it dry and shrink for two weeks. The pomander ball should be kept in an open, sunny spot in your home throughout this period.

When the pomander ball has finished drying, it is time to decorate it with ribbons, lace, or netting. Wrap a colorful ribbon (or lace or netting) around the middle of the orange and tie a double knot at the top of the orange. Then, wrap another ribbon around the orange in the other direction (dividing the orange into quarters) and tie a double knot again at the top of the orange and tie on a pretty *favour* (bow).

If you would like to hang the pomander, attach a loop of ribbon to this topknot. Or, you can simply place the pomander back in a bowl to make any space in your house smell absolutely delicious.

On a Garden Path. Two springs passed and William grew into an active toddler. In the company of his parents beneath the protective shade of the yellow honeysuckle, William no doubt delighted in his first small steps and was enchanted by the beauty and smells of the herbs and flowers in the garden.

And as William grew older, he would take walks in the country. Later, while writing his sonnets and plays, he would recall that

> daisies pied, and violets blue,
> And lady-smocks all silver white,
> And cuckoo-buds of yellow hue
> Do paint the meadows with delight;
> daffodils . . . take [charm] the winds of March with beauty;
> of all flowers . . . a rose is best.

As William matured, he also observed how useful herbs and flowers could be. His mother used them not only to flavor foods but also to make wines, scent her cupboards and floors, and treat illnesses and pains. When used as medicine, these herbs were called simples.

In the first four lines of one of Shakespeare's sonnets (number 18 of 154), he compares a person to the summertime. Notice his use of the word *temperate* in line two:

> Shall I compare thee to a summer's day?
> Thou art more lovely and more temperate:
> Rough winds do shake the darling buds of May,
> And summer's lease hath all too short a date . . .

In other words, this person is much better than summer!

A Flower a Month

Shakespeare was born in April. Which flower represents the month you were born in?

- January: Snowdrop
- February: Primrose
- March: Violet
- April: Daisy
- May: Hawthorn
- June: Rose
- July: Water Lily
- August: Poppy
- September: Morning Glory
- October: Hops
- November: Chrysanthemum
- December: Holly

Definitions

Pied means in a variety of colors.

Thou and *thee* mean you. *Date* means duration.

ACT 1, SCENE 2 John Shakespeare supports his growing family.

1569: Two Houses—Both Alike in Busyness. The Shakespeares's two houses on Henley Street were bustling! Mary Arden Shakespeare was now the mother of William (5), Gilbert (3), and Joan (a baby). As Joan was swinging 'round and 'round in the baby-minder in the middle of the living room, Gilbert was enjoying spinning his top. He also liked the sound that his parents' gold and silver coins made when they jingle-jangled together. Meanwhile, William was busy learning ABCs in petty school, which was similar to a modern kindergarten. While her children were occupied, Mary focused on chores: cooking, sewing, cleaning, farming, and gardening. Someday, Mary's daughter would join her in these chores while her sons attended school. (Only daughters of wealthy people—such as Queen Elizabeth I—received a complete education, including lessons in foreign languages and arithmetic.) Despite all the demands of being a working mother, Mary still must have felt very blessed.

Like his wife, John Shakespeare was very busy. This native son of farmers from the nearby village of Snitterfield was now the father of three children. As an entrepreneur, he provided well for his family. He was not only a *whittawer* (someone who transforms hides into white leather) and *glover* (someone who makes gloves) but also a dealer in timber, barley, and wool. Each Wednesday must have been especially hectic for John because that was the day before he would take his leather gloves, purses, aprons, and belts to sell at market.

Since the twelfth century, Thursdays in Stratford-upon-Avon, the regional center for trade, came alive with friendly exchange between farmers and townspeople. There were so many things to buy: meat, butter, barley, corn, cheese, eggs, fruit, cloth, shoes, sugar, tools, clothing, horses, calves, and sheep! The marketplace, bursting with colors, aromas, and noises, would once again be overwhelming for all of the senses—in every sense of the word!

In addition to his roles as husband, father, and businessman, John Shakespeare also served on the town council of his adopted hometown. From 1556 to 1568, John rose from ale-taster to constable to burgess to alderman to the highest elected office, bailiff (mayor), which he held for the standard period of one year. Every morning, burgesses, aldermen, the bailiff, and the town clerk met to run the newly chartered borough's business. As citizens of an incorporated town, they were responsible for the school, the teacher's salary (20 pounds per year), Clopton Bridge, the chapel, the market, fairs, roads, and they also handled disputes between residents and helped to administer the Poor Laws, which required that the wealthy assist in supporting the poor of their town (almost half of their population was poor in 1601).

John Shakespeare signed documents with a cross or his mark, a pair of glover's compasses (tools of his trade). Just because he didn't spell out his name doesn't mean he couldn't read and write, for many literate men signed with only their marks. In either case, as a citizen of Stratford, William Shakespeare's father was a respected and popular man.

Decorate a Pair of Gloves

s a master glover and tanner, John Shakespeare undoubtedly began his career as an apprentice to learn the science and art of his trade. After seven years of on-the-job training—making white leather out of the hides of horses, deer, hounds, goats, and sheep—John Shakespeare eventually opened his own shop.

Other tradesman in town formed and joined guilds, or companies, as was customary in incorporated towns. But the Glovers Guild was not formed until 1606, five years after John Shakespeare died. Had he lived, he would have unquestionably been a valued and respected member.

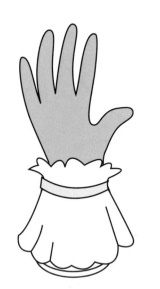

Gloves could be made simply or they could be lined with fur, decorated with ribbons, lace, and tassles, or even perfumed. Why not try your hand at making a dressy pair?

Materials

❋ Measuring tape

❋ 1 yard of 2- to 4-inch-wide lace

❋ Scissors

❋ 1 pair of leather gloves. (To determine your size, measure the area across your palm, excluding your thumb, and double that measurement. That is your glove size. If you don't own a pair of leather gloves that you can decorate, visit a thrift shop for a selection of inexpensive gloves. For the sake of authenticity, white leather would be the color of choice, but any color will do.)

❋ Masking tape

❋ Hot glue gun with glue-gun sticks

Adult help suggested.

Measure your wrist and add a couple of inches to that number. Cut a corresponding amount of lace.

Position the glove on a handle or spool so you can work with the glove using both of your hands.

Wrap the lace around the glove, securing it as you go with masking tape for positioning purposes only.

When you've finished wrapping, pull back the edge of the lace and, working your way around with the glue, secure the lace to the leather. Peel back the masking tape as you go.

If you'd like, for extra flair, make six evenly distanced cuts halfway up the band of lace.

The cuff for the glove you've just made is called a *gauntlet*.

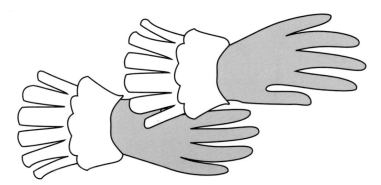

act 1, scene 3 John Shakespeare takes his son to see his first play.

1569: A Spark Is Ignited. One day, a troupe of performers arrived in Stratford to entertain the townspeople. As bailiff, John Shakespeare was required to preview and censor any play before the citizens of the town could see it. Thus, the Guildhall, where the town council met, was quickly converted into a playhouse. Apparently, John liked what he saw because he gave them permission to perform there for the town and paid the players nine shillings.

Strolling players travelled throughout England.

In addition to his first play and the other plays he saw in Stratford as he grew up, it is likely that William and his family enjoyed juggling shows, mystery and miracle plays, and the *Corpus Christi* play performed in nearby Coventry each June. It's also probable that he and his family attended a portion of the 18-day-long pageant and water show held for Queen Elizabeth I on the grounds of Robert Dudley's (the Earl of Leicester) castle in 1575—complete with fireworks and cannon fire! William was certainly born at the perfect time—when entertainment was lord of the manor!

Payment authorized by John Shakespeare for the performing troupe in 1569

Robert Dudley, the Earl of Leicester

Learn How to Juggle

Jugglers were a vivid part of the Elizabethan landscape. Fairs, festivals, and celebrations often included jugglers who, with their colorful costumes and special tricks, delighted children and adults alike.

Materials

❋ 3 brightly colored beanbags, each one a different color—red, yellow, and blue, for example—squeezable, but not too firm. Alternatively, you can use rolled-up socks. Optional: Three small, lightweight chiffon scarves—each one a different color

One beanbag: Keep your hands between your waist and your chest when throwing and catching. To do this, imagine your hands are holding up a rectangular window frame. Your right hand is holding up the bottom right-hand corner. The two imaginary points you will be tossing toward are the top right and left corners of the window's frame. Your hands will be tossing the beanbags up and across in a slight scooping motion, as if you were scooping and tossing sand or a handful of leaves into the air. The path of the beanbag will form an arc. Toss the red one up toward the imaginary corner on the left and catch it with the left hand. Let the beanbag fall into your hand. With practice, you will not have to move your hand too much to toss or catch the beanbag. Now, toss and catch the beanbag beginning with your left hand. Continue to do this until you feel comfortable with the back-and-forth motion. When you have mastered tossing and catching one beanbag, you will be ready to move on to two beanbags.

Two beanbags: Next, with the red one in your right hand and the yellow one in the other, toss the red one. When the red one reaches the peak of the arc, release the yellow one by throwing it up and inside the path of the red one. Then catch the red one with your left hand and then catch the yellow one with your right hand. Continue tossing and catching. Perhaps it would be helpful to say these words to yourself as you practice: toss, toss, catch, catch, toss, toss, catch, catch.

Helpful Hint

You might feel more comfortable beginning with small, lightweight scarves. Scarves are lighter than beanbags and take longer to fall, which gives you more time to get used to the juggling motion. Once you are at ease juggling with scarves, you will be ready to begin juggling with the beanbags.

Three beanbags—The Cascade. Hold the red and blue beanbags in your right hand. The red beanbag should be cradled between the second and third fingers and your thumb. The blue beanbag is held below it and to the left beneath your ring and finger and pinky.

Round one:
1. Right hand tosses red into the air

2. As red is reaching its peak, toss yellow into the air with the left hand
3. Left hand catches red
4. Right hand tosses blue
5. Right hand catches yellow

The sequence is right toss, left toss, left catch, right toss (third beanbag), right catch

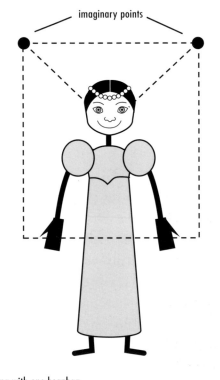

imaginary points

right left

catch

Juggling with one beanbag

Round two:

6. Left hand tosses red into air

7. Left hand catches blue

8. Right hand tosses yellow

9. Right hand catches red

10. Left hand tosses blue

11. Left hand catches yellow

Round three: pattern begins again

At first, you will probably only be able to toss and catch one or two complete rounds. You will surely drop a few, and a beanbag may even hit you on the head after it collides in midair with another one. This may happen often in the beginning. But don't worry. With practice, juggling will eventually become easier for you. As your hands and eyes work together faster, you will be able to lower the cascade pattern to eyeball height or below.

It's a Small World. There were four social classes and within each class were more divisions. The four basic classes were gentleman, citizen, yeoman (small landowner), and laborer. Mary Arden Shakespeare, the youngest of eight daughters, was born to a gentleman farmer and raised in Wilmcote (about three miles from Stratford). In addition to their property in Wilmcote, Mary's father also owned over 100 acres with two farmhouses in Snitterfield. Coincidentally, when William's parents, John and Mary, were growing up, John's father rented his home and a portion of his farming land in Snitterfield from Mary's father!

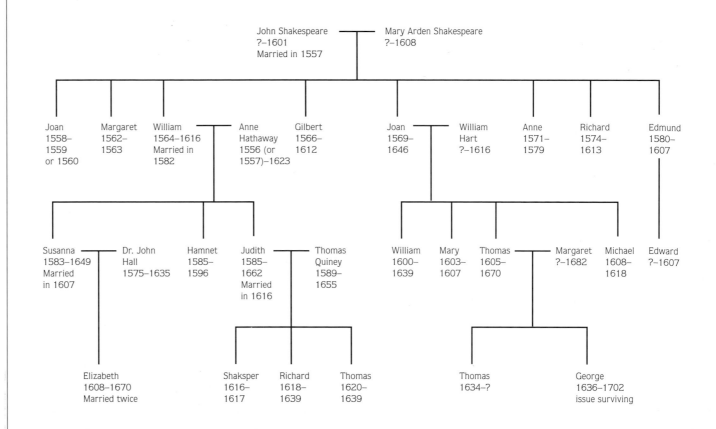

The Shakespeare family tree bears fruit.

Your Own Family Tree

Interesting stories about your family can be discovered by creating a family tree. Use the Shakespeare tree as an example.

Materials
* Paper or poster board large enough to write down all the names and dates
* Pencil
* Ruler

To begin, write "Mother's Side of the Family" on the upper left-hand corner of your paper and write "Father's Side of the Family" on the upper right-hand corner. Use your ruler to divide your paper in half with a line drawn from top to bottom.

Your grandparents' generation: Near the top of the page, on the left-hand side of the sheet, write down the names of your mother's parents next to each other. Near the top of the page, on the right-hand side of the sheet, write the names of your father's parents next to each other. Connect each pair of names with a horizontal line.

Your parents' generation: Draw a small vertical line from the middle of both horizontal lines that you drew between your two sets of grandparents, and then draw two horizontal lines—as many inches across as you think you'll need to list the names of your mother, her brothers and sisters, their husbands and wives, and your father, his brothers and sisters, and their husbands and wives (your aunts and uncles). Place your parents' names on the appropriate side of the chart to the right and left of the center line, which you drew earlier.

Your generation: Draw a horizontal line between your parents (and their siblings and spouses). Draw vertical lines down from the middle of each of these lines, and then draw horizontal lines again, as many inches across as you think you'll need to list your name, your brothers' and sisters' names, and the names of your first cousins.

act 1, scene 4 According to Shakespeare, attending school was the second of the seven ages of man.

School Days. Although there is no written evidence that William attended King Edward VI's New School, it is supposed that William, as the son of an alderman, was a participating student.

The Early Bird. A mama bird shook off the last droplet of rain from her feathers. With startling speed, she darted from a tree in the Shakespeare garden to gather food for her young. The songbirds were making a considerable racket this morning. William probably wished he were back home upstairs in his nest, with his eyes tightly shut, snug in the warmth of his featherbed. *Well-a-day* (alas), today was a school day, so there was no choice in the matter. Dawn was approaching, and the light of the glowworm was disappearing with each dewdrop. Walking on the partially paved streets, muddy from last night's storm, made the short trip very difficult—and messy! Thus, William was, as were probably his friends Richard Quiney, William Reynolds, and Richard Tyler, *creeping like snail unwillingly to school.*

Tudor desk, Shakespeare's birthplace

'Tis the Mind That Makes the Body Rich. Would Stratford-upon-Avon's children have *brain*[s]... *as dry as the remainder* [leftover] *biscuit after a voyage* or *not so much brain as earwax?* Or, with the right education, would they flower into worthwhile and generous countrymen the borough could be proud of? The answer to that question was decided many years before William was born: From the late thirteenth century onward, Stratford had been educating its young men for future study at the universities and service to the town. William and his schoolmates were just more boys in a long line of potential *literati* (that's Latin for "scholarly people").

King Edward VI New School

It was in school where William learned about people from the past—real and imagined—and where language came alive! One of the Latin books that William read in school was *Zodiacus Vitae (Zodiac of Life)* by Renaissance poet Palingenius, which provided him with the inspiration for his famous speech:

> All the world's a stage,
> And all the men and women merely players;
> They have their exits and their entrances,
> And one man in his time plays many parts,
> His acts being seven ages.

As young William was reading his Latin texts in school, businessman James Burbage (a former carpenter-turned-actor/entrepreneur) was building the first outdoor playhouse called The Theatre just north of London's city limits. (The first indoor playhouse had been built for him in 1567, called The Red Lion.) Within 11 years, two more theaters, The Curtain and The Rose, would join it and forever change London, the theater world, and literature. The dramatic arts had found a permanent home at last. Of course, William probably did not even know about this progress—nor did he know what effect the opening of these theaters in London would have on his life beginning just a decade later.

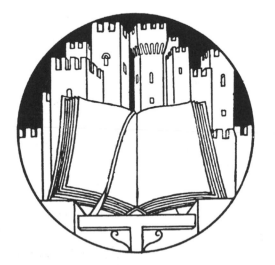

Create a Habitat for Birds

Stratford-upon-Avon boasted many trees, including 1,000 elms, and their branches were home to thousands of birds. William undoubtedly loved to watch them fly about as he listened to their songs. In his plays, he referred to birds often and, quite naturally, poetically.

The use of two songbirds in *Romeo and Juliet* shows Shakespeare's poetic weaving of birds, time, and love. The scene occurs the morning after Romeo has been banished from Verona for killing Juliet's cousin, Tybalt. Romeo must now leave Juliet and the city of Verona immediately. In this scene, Juliet tells her Romeo that the song they have just heard was the nightingale's nighttime melody, which means that he does not have to leave yet, and not the morning lark's tune, which would mean he must leave.

Juliet:

> Wilt thou be gone? it is not yet near day.
> It was the nightingale, and not the lark,
> That pierced the fearful hollow of thine ear;
> Nightly she sings on yond pomegranate tree.
> Believe me, love, it was the nightingale.

Romeo:

> It was the lark, the herald of the morn,
> No nightingale. Look, love, what envious streaks
> Do lace the severing clouds in yonder east.
> Night's candles are burnt out, and jocund day
> Stands tiptoe on the misty mountain tops.
> I must be gone and live, or stay and die.

If you've ever seen a robin's nest filled with baby-blue eggs in your yard and then experienced the excitement of watching them hatch, eat, and learn how to fly, then you already know how spectacular nature can be! Creating a backyard habitat for birds is fun and rewarding. You can be more observant of birds by creating a welcome habitat for birds in your own backyard.

For the Birds

Sunflower kernels attract the widest variety of birds. Avoid the sunflower shells because they're messy. Thistle seeds attract finches. Use safflower seeds if you don't want to attract the larger birds.

Common North American birds to watch for are chickadee, wren, cardinal, towhee, red-winged blackbird, chipping sparrow, field sparrow, song sparrow, junco, white-throated sparrow, mourning dove, nuthatch, woodpecker, hummingbird, jay, evening grosbeak, goldfinch, pine siskin, purple finch, and house finch.

Materials

❋ Pencil
❋ Paper
❋ Bird feeder (See instructions below.)
❋ Variety of bird food—seeds, suet, or nectar (Recipes for suet and nectar follow.)
❋ Water source

Optional

❋ Binoculars
❋ Field guide (a picture book of birds)

Draw a picture of your backyard with a pencil and paper and identify and label the names of the trees and shrubs already in place. An adult might be able to help you with this step. These trees and shrubs are called "cover," and cover is important because it provides birds protection from other animals and the weather. In addition, cover provides food in the form of berries, seeds, and nuts. Don't forget to include a water source or a pedestal birdbath. Place it in the open in a sunny location. Add fresh water every day and clean the bath once a week.

You can learn about birds from encyclopedias, library books, the Internet, field guides about birds, or talking with bird-watchers.

Remember to place bird feeders where you can comfortably watch the birds from a window in your home without disturbing them. Some feeders attach to your house or to your windows and some attach to poles. If you have a pet cat or dog, you shouldn't place the feeder so low that your pet interferes with the birds' feeding time. Bird feeders should be cleaned frequently.

Build a Bird Feeder or Nesting Shelf

Materials

❀ Plastic 1-gallon milk container, empty

❀ Scissors

❀ 20 inches of wire

Adult help suggested.

Wash the milk container with soap and water. Dry thoroughly.

Cut two four- by four-inch holes—one across from the other—about two inches from the bottom of the plastic container.

Make two small holes at the top of the container and run the wire through the holes. Use this wire to hang the bird feeder or nesting shelf from a branch of a tree. The bird feeder or nesting shelf should be hung at least four feet above ground.

For the nesting shelf only: Poke about four small holes into the bottom of the container for ventilation and drainage.

For the bird feeder only: Fill the container about one inch deep with sunflower kernels.

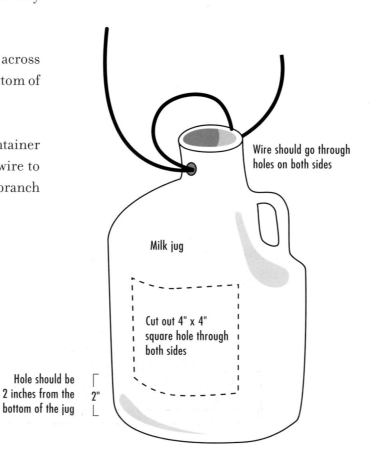

Wire should go through holes on both sides

Milk jug

Cut out 4" x 4" square hole through both sides

Hole should be 2 inches from the bottom of the jug — 2"

Feed the Birds

SUET RECIPE

Suet attracts mockingbirds, woodpeckers, and songbirds.

Ingredients
❋ 1 cup chunky peanut butter
❋ 2 cups vegetable shortening
❋ 1 cup flour
❋ 1 cup rolled oats
❋ 1 cup coarse corn meal
❋ 1 cup hulled sunflower seeds
❋ Crushed egg shells

Utensils
❋ Spoon
❋ Bowl

Mix together all ingredients. Add extra flour and cornmeal until mixture reaches cookie-dough consistency. Shape the suet into a log or spread it directly on tree bark.

EASTERN HUMMINGBIRD NECTAR RECIPE

Ingredients
❋ 1 cup white sugar
❋ 4 cups water

Utensils
❋ Spoon
❋ Pot
❋ Hummingbird feeder
Adult help suggested.

Add the sugar to the water and bring to a boil. Boil for 5 minutes. Store surplus in the refrigerator.

Do not use honey, artificial sweeteners, or food coloring in the nectar. Because nectar ferments quickly, you must clean the nectar feeder and refill it with fresh nectar every day. If you don't do this, the birds will become sick. Clean the outside of the feeder regularly with a damp towel. This will help prevent the feeder from attracting bees and wasps.

The Guildhall and the Grammar School

A Hard Day's Work. Gone were William's days of petty school and learning from a "hornbook," or lesson tablet, which kept William's younger siblings busy. While the five- to six-year-old boys—and sometimes girls—studied ABCs, cursive writing, reading, religious material, and simple arithmetic with the "usher" (assistant to the teacher), seven- to fourteen-year-old schoolboys like William endured a much harder day with a university-educated teacher.

The school day was extremely long. During the spring and summer, the children were seated by six o'clock in the morning and were not dismissed until five o'clock in the afternoon. In the fall and winter, when the days were shorter, school began at seven o'clock in the morning and lasted until four o'clock in the afternoon.

Only on Thursdays and Saturdays did school end early—at noon. Thursdays were market days and Saturdays were set aside for bathing and doing laundry.

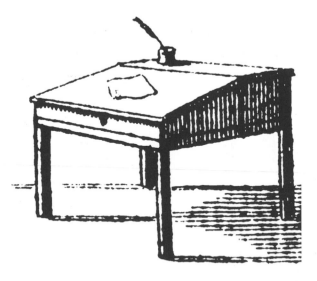

A Hornbook

When William was five years old, he and his schoolmates learned the alphabet with the aid of a hornbook, which was an alphabet tablet made of oak. A leaf of paper or parchment imprinted with the ABCs and a prayer was covered with a thin sheet of transparent horn. The horn was nailed down at each corner, making this learning tool almost indestructible. As Shakespearean scholar Anthony Burgess put it, the hornbook was "a kind of wooden spade for feeding knowledge to the young."

You can make a hornbook and dramatize this part of school life as it was in England until the end of the 18th century.

Materials

* Cardboard, 12 inches long by 6 inches wide
* Pencil
* Ruler
* Scissors
* Sheet of white writing paper, 8½ by 11 inches, cut in half so it measures 8½ by 5½ inches
* 4 brass fasteners
* Double-sided tape
* Plastic page protector or clear contact paper
* Heavy-duty hole puncher

Adult help suggested.

Horn-book

Draw a rectangle 9 inches long by 6 inches wide on the sheet of cardboard. Next, draw a handle of 3 inches long by 2 inches wide at the bottom center of this rectangle.

Cut along the lines you have drawn and then set aside this spade-shaped cardboard.

Prepare your lesson sheet on the writing paper.

Center your lesson sheet on the cardboard pad- dle. Attach it at the top and bottom with the double-sided tape.

Cut a plastic page protector or clear contact paper into a rectangle 9 inches long by 6 inches wide. Align this page protector on top of the card-board paddle.

Punch 4 holes into the corners of your hornbook and insert the fasteners into these holes. Now you are ready to begin your reading drills!

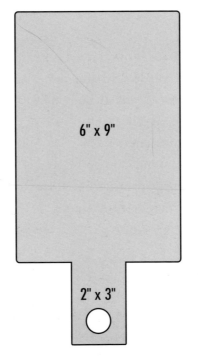

6" x 9"

2" x 3"

abcdefgh
ijklmnop
qrstuvwxyz
ABCDEFGH
IJKLMNOP
QRSTUV
WXYZ

In His Mind's Eye. William endured long hours of study at school. Because there was little time for fun, it's easy to imagine that he daydreamed now and then about swimming in the Avon or practicing archery over by Clopton Bridge. He probably could not wait for holiday fairs and weekly market days. Acrobats, jugglers, musicians, singers, and scenes from the life of Robin Hood or St. George (the patron saint of England) were certainly amusing for people of all ages. And the food vendors' fruit pies and gingerbreads made those days even more special for the townspeople and farmers who worked and studied so hard throughout the year.

Recess. *Out of doubt* (surely), William and his schoolmates looked forward to breaks for breakfast at 9 A.M., lunch from 11 A.M. to 1 P.M., and perhaps an occasional late afternoon recess—time to *gambol* (skip), run, and play cards, hide-and-seek, and leapfrog. What a relief these fun activities must have been from the work that filled the school hours day in and day out: translating Latin into English and English into Latin; memorizing Latin texts; reciting speeches and poetry; singing psalms; learning ethics from Aesop (for example, "Don't count your chickens before they are hatched"); performing dramas; and studying literature, history, logic, French, Greek, vocabulary, and Latin grammar.

Although Sundays were somewhat of a weekly holiday from school when families were required to attend church and listen to the stories from the Bible, they weren't entirely free days because the master would quiz the boys on the parish minister's sermon afterward!

A Little Bit of This, A Little Bit of That. Elizabethans washed their hands and said prayers before and after every meal. Lunch was eaten between 11 A.M. and noon. Supper, the largest meal of the day, was served between 6 P.M. and 9 P.M. Elizabethans enjoyed combinations of whole wheat bread, butter, milk, eggs, nuts, vegetables, cheese, fruit, cake, pie, stew, beef, mutton, chicken, salad (greens mixed with fruits, nuts, and flowers), and fish. To help England's fishing and shipbuilding industries flourish, meat was forbidden on Wednesdays, Fridays, and Saturdays.

And what about something to drink? Unfortunately, water was not very clean, and tea, the drink most associated with England—tea and crumpets, tea and scones, teatime!—would not be introduced until the 17th century. So ale, which contained little alcohol, was the drink of choice for adults and children alike.

Perhaps you'll enjoy this recipe for Apple Moye.

An Observation from Shakespeare:

Unquiet meals make ill digestions.

In other words, to ensure that each mealtime is pleasant, have a sunny disposition!

Apple Moye

Here is the recipe as it was written in Elizabethan times:

Take Apples, and cut them in two or foure peeces, boyle them till they be soft, and bruise them in a morter, and put thereto the yolks of two Eggs, and a litle sweet butter, set them on a chafingdish of coales, and boyle them a litle, and put thereto a litle Sugar, synamon and Ginger, and so serve them in.

Here's the modern version of this recipe.

Ingredients

* ❊ 8–10 apples
* ❊ ¼ cup water
* ❊ 2 egg yolks
* ❊ 2 tablespoons butter
* ❊ 1 teaspoon cinnamon
* ❊ 1 teaspoon ground ginger
* ❊ ½ cup sugar

Utensils

* ❊ Knife
* ❊ Saucepan
* ❊ Fork
* ❊ Glass measuring cup
* ❊ Measuring spoons

Adult help suggested.

Peel and core the apples, quarter them, and place them in a saucepan with the water. Bring to a boil, then simmer for about 20 minutes or until tender. Mash the apples with a fork and blend in the egg yolks, butter, spices, and sugar. Cook over a very low heat, stirring occasionally, for another 10 minutes.

Serve hot or chilled.

Serves 4 to 6 people.

Optional: You might want to serve this sweet apple dish with ice cream, frozen yogurt, or sorbet. Garnish with cookies.

Eat No Onions Nor Garlic, for We Are to Utter Sweet Breath. Although the Elizabethans cleaned their teeth by rubbing them with a linen cloth and a liquid or powder, unpleasant breath was still a problem. And Shakespeare's lines about breath show that he could write not only about noble and beautiful experiences but also about everyday, down-to-earth occurrences. Here are some less-than-dainty remarks you might find amusing.

From *Henry VI, Part II*:

His breath stinks with eating toasted cheese.

From *Measure for Measure*:

[You have] a blasting and a scandalous breath.

From *Julius Caesar*:

The rabblement howted, and clapp'd their chopped hands, and threw up their sweaty night-caps, and uttered such a deal of stinking breath . . . that it had, almost, choked Caesar.

Definitions

Howted means cheered.

Chopped means chapped.

Create New Words

illiam Shakespeare coined many words and used familiar words in new ways. For example, thanks to his love of language, we have the nouns:

alligator (from the Spanish *el lagarto*)
anchovy (from the Spanish *anchova*)
critic (from the Greek *krinein*)
embrace (from the Middle French *embracer*)

not to mention these nouns: eyeball, farmhouse, fortune-teller, glow, hint, luggage, manager, moonbeam, mountaineer, puppy dog, scuffle, shooting star, skim milk, tardiness, urging, watchdog, and wild-goose chase;

the adjectives: full-grown, green-eyed, laughable, lonely, madcap, majestic, olympian, snail-paced, softhearted, unreal, varied, well-behaved, and worthless;

the verbs: gossip, hurry, mimic, numb, partner, petition, puke, and undress;

and the adverbs: downstairs, importantly, instinctively, threateningly, tightly, and vastly.

You, too, can combine existing words to create new words, use a word in a new way, or simply coin a new word from another language!

Materials

❋ Dictionary
❋ Thesaurus
❋ Paper
❋ Pencil or pen
❋ Your imagination

Create a new word by combining or splicing together two or more existing words. Here are a few ideas to get you started:

1. Make up a word describing a title of a book, play, or movie that is "snappy" and "catchy."
2. Make up the name of a movie that has it all—comedy, drama, adventure, and romance.
3. Make up a word for what it's called when a person talks to animals.

Possible new words:

1. snatchy
2. CARD: an acronym for comedy, adventure, romance, and drama!
3. dolittling (Inspired by the book *Dr. Dolittle*, about a doctor who talks to animals)

In the future, if you need a new word to describe a person, place, or thing, don't wait for someone else to create it—invent it yourself! After all, it's your language too!

And speaking of length, the longest word in Shakespeare's plays is *honorificabilitudinitatibus*. Try saying that trippingly on the tongue! This word can be found in *Love's Labour's Lost*, and, as you may have already guessed, it means "honorableness."

Definitions

In drama, a soliloquy is a speech in which the character speaks alone to the audience and reveals his innermost thoughts and feelings. The other characters in the play are completely unaware of these remarks. The word *soliloquy* comes from Latin: *soli* meaning "alone" and *loqu(i)* meaning "(to) speak."

It's Play Time! As you can see, William Shakespeare made up many English words and phrases and often used an existing word in a new way. Another word he made up is *trippingly* (lightly, easily).

His character, Hamlet, the Prince of Denmark, uses *trippingly* when he commands the players in the play he is staging to

> Speak the speech, I pray you, as I pronounc'd it to
> you, trippingly on the tongue . . .

Why is Prince Hamlet putting on a play? Because he wants to find out if the ghost of his murdered father is telling him the truth. Did Prince Hamlet's Uncle Claudius—who is now the King and his stepfather (he married Hamlet's mother!)—kill Hamlet's father? If Claudius did kill Hamlet's father, then when he hears certain lines in the play about a murder, his reaction should reveal his guilt or innocence. And, if guilty, then Hamlet might be able to avenge his father's death, as is the ghost's wish.

> Does Hamlet fulfill the ghost's wish? To find out . . .

> Read or watch the play and you will see
> What is *to be or not to be*!

If someone tells you that he is going to play the part of Hamlet, be sure to let him know you are impressed. Why? Of Shakespeare's 1,277 characters, Hamlet has the biggest part: 1,530 lines and 11,610 words. In fact, the play itself is the longest of his 38 plays: It has 4,042 lines and 29,551 words. The soliloquy (see sidebar) that begins "To be or not to be" has 260 words alone. Did you know that it is this speech that the *Guinness Book of World Records* judges use to determine the world's fastest talker? The record for 1995 is 23.8 seconds. This is equivalent to 650 words per minute!

Most of Shakespeare's plays were adapted from legends, plays, and poems. *Hamlet* was based on the legend of Amleth or Amlotha, a Danish nobleman who avenged his father's death. *Hamlet* was written from about 1599 to 1601, which was around the time of William's father's death in September 1601.

A Man of Fire-New Words. William had fun with language. His use of hyperbole, simile, metaphor, and personification coupled with a vocabulary of 29 thousand words electrified the theatrical experience. With over 33 thousand references, he is the most-quoted author in the *Oxford English Dictionary*. You use Shakespeare's words and phrases every day and probably don't even realize it!

Just like Shakespeare, you can create pictures with words. But first, you should know what hyperbole, simile, metaphor, and personification mean.

Hyperbole:
Exaggeration:

> Purple the sails, and so perfumed that
> The winds were lovesick with them . . .

Simile:
Comparing one thing to something else by using *like* or *as:*

> O, she doth teach the torches to burn bright!
> It seems she hangs upon the cheek of night
> Like a rich jewel in an Ethiop's ear.

Metaphor:
Comparing one thing to something else without using *like* or *as* (the comparison is implied):

> But soft, what light through yonder window breaks?
> It is the east, and Juliet is the sun.

Personification:
Giving an inanimate thing a life or personality:

> But look, the morn in russet mantle clad
> Walks o'er the dew of yon high eastward hill.

Bethump'd with Words. An oxymoron is a combining of words opposite in meaning. The phrase *freezing fire* is an example. Writers pair these opposites to startle you or to make you really think. Shakespeare's use of this device reflects the playfulness with which he approached language and his appreciation of life's mysteries. At first, these pairings seem contradictory, but upon closer examination, they reveal a certain truth.

Opposites Attract: Oxymorons

Definitions

In this verse, *vanity* means worthlessness and *smoke* means the color gray.

The following verse from *Romeo and Juliet* contains 10 oxymorons. See if you can pick the oxymoron pairs out. Write them down and then compare your list to the list of oxymoron pairs that follow.

Materials
* Paper
* Pencil
* Your imagination

In this verse, Romeo speaks about his unrequited love for a girl named Rosaline (He hasn't met Juliet yet).

Romeo:

> Alas that love, whose view is muffled still,
> Should, without eyes, see pathways to his will!
> Where shall we dine? O me! what fray was here?
> Yet tell me not, for I have heard it all:

Here's much to do with hate, but more with love.
Why then, O brawling love! O loving hate!
O any thing, of nothing first create!
O heavy lightness, serious vanity,
Misshapen chaos of well-seeming forms,
Feather of lead, bright smoke, cold fire, sick health,
Still-waking sleep, that is not what it is!
This love feel I, that feel no love in this.

brawling / love
loving / hate
heavy / lightness
serious / vanity
misshapen chaos / well-seeming forms
feather / lead
bright / smoke
cold / fire
sick / health
still-waking / sleep

Now that you're familiar with oxymorons, try combining these words to make your own interesting pairs:

beautiful	lamb
damned	fiend
raven	honorable
wolvish-ravening	saint
dove-feathered	angelical
tyrant	villain

Now see what oxymorons Shakespeare's Juliet created from these words. In this scene, Juliet learns that her husband, Romeo, has been banished from Verona for killing her cousin Tybalt. See if you can find Juliet's oxymorons.

Juliet:

> O serpent heart, hid with a flow'ring face!
> Did ever dragon keep so fair a cave?
> Beautiful tyrant! fiend angelical!
> Dove-feathered raven! wolvish ravening lamb!
> Despised substance of divinest show!
> Just opposite to what thou justly seem'st,
> A damned saint, an honorable villain!
> O nature, what hadst thou to do in hell
> When thou didst bower the spirit of a fiend
> In mortal paradise of such sweet flesh?

> Was ever book containing such vile matter
> So fairly bound? O that deceit should dwell
> In such a gorgeous palace!

DAYS of LOVE and LEAVING MARRIAGE and FAMILY

rom 1578 through 1585. William Shakespeare finishes school, marries Anne Hathaway, becomes a father, and departs for the writing life in London.

act 2, scene 1 At home on Henley Street.

Kitchen of the Shakespeare home on Henley Street.
Notice the "baby minder" in the foreground.

What Next? When William turned 14 or so, his father began having financial troubles. Regrettably, John Shakespeare also had to give up his seat on the town council (which he would not regain until 1601, the year he died). Although he never lost his homes on Henley Street or his fellow citizens' respect, his finances began to dwindle and he no longer attended church for fear of being arrested because of the money he owed. Consequently, he was unable to send William on to Oxford or Cambridge. Luckily, as it turned out, being unable to afford a university education proved not to be a monumental loss for William or the theater world.

aCT 2, SCeNe 2 In Shottery, England.

A Little Romance? William, a teenager, and Anne Hathaway, eight years older than he, began their courtship in the summer of 1582. When did they fall in love? Sadly, we don't know the details of their courtship. However, if we choose to romanticize history, we can even invent a little story, à la Shakespeare . . .

Not yet old enough for a man nor young enough for a boy, with *the rose of youth upon him*, eighteen-year-old William looked forward to his walks over the grassy fields the mile or so to Anne's farm in Shottery. One Saturday, walking purposefully with a sonnet in his heart, he composed a poem for her. And later that afternoon, they dangled their feet in a babbling brook and shared a scrumptious fruit pie. Throughout that summer, they continued to meet by the brook, in the fields of Shottery, and on the courting bench near her fireplace, which remains there still.

Unfortunately, no love letters, no diaries, no mementos exist to illuminate their courtship. All that is actually understood is that by November of 1582, William, who was under 21 and, therefore, underage, had to ask for permission from his parents to marry Anne, who was 26.

Instead of marrying in Anne's parish and registering the occasion there, they received a license to marry from a special court in the town of Worcester, requiring only one of the three announcements to be read in church before the wedding. (It was the custom to announce upcoming marriages in church on three separate occasions to give people the opportunity to object to the marriage. For instance, if the bride or groom were already married, obviously, the wedding could not take place.) Before long, William and Anne received a blessing—their daughter Susanna was born. And two years after Susanna's birth, in 1585, twins, Hamnet and Judith, were born.

The buttery inside Anne Hathaway's cottage

Anne Hathaway's cottage

The living room inside Anne Hathaway's cottage

The baptismal records of Hamnet and Judith

A Family Man. By 1583, Mary and John Shakespeare still had four children living with them at home. With William's family no doubt living there too, the Shakespeare's extended family now consisted of nine members—not to mention any servants and apprentices who may have also lived with them. And, by 1585, the arrival of the twins enlarged the household to 11!

Christening

Elizabethan Games

It is interesting to imagine that during *after-supper* (a light meal or dessert served after a big meal), before the last embers of the blaze were extinguished in their brick and stone fireplace, William read *antique fables* (fanciful tales) and told stories full of history, humor, drama, and romance to his family. It is also likely that their evenings and Saturday and Sunday afternoons were filled with laughter and games. After all, the Elizabethans loved recreation. With bowling, singing, reading aloud, chess, cards, tag, plays, and leapfrog, there were many activities to keep this growing family busy.

Teetotum

Toys called "tops," which had been popular since Greek and Roman times, reached England by the 1300s. One particular four-sided spinning top called a *teetotum* was twirled with the fingers by spinning the spindle that ran through it. Whether simply watching it whirl around on a flat surface or playing the following game, the teetotum undoubtedly provided hours of fun for Elizabethan children of all ages.

Materials
* 4-sided wooden top
* Pen
* Markers—pennies, beans, or wrapped candy (something to put in the "pot")

Mark each side of the top: T for take, N for nothing, P for put, and H for half. Two or more players sit on the floor or at a table.

Distribute the markers (at least 10), giving each player the same amount.

To begin the game, everyone puts 1 marker into the center. This is called the pot.

The object of the game is to win all the other players' markers or the most markers at the end of a certain amount of time. (You decide this.)

The first player spins the top. What happens next depends on which side of the top is showing:

If T (take): the player takes the whole pot. Then, everyone puts 1 more marker into the pot, and the game continues.

If N (nothing): the player can quit and walk away from the game with the markers she still has or she can choose to do nothing—take nothing and put nothing into the pot.

If P (put): the player adds a marker to the pot.

If H (half): the player takes half the pot. If the pot has an odd number of markers, decide if the player should take more than half or one less than half of the number of markers. This decision should be made before the game begins. If there is only one marker

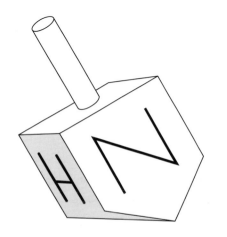

in the pot, and a player spins an H, play that spin as if it had landed on N—do nothing.

Continue spinning the top and doing as the top tells you.

Then, at the end of the game, the player with the most markers wins!

Nine Men's Morris

The Elizabethans played Nine Men's Morris the way it is described below. But during Renaissance pageants, they also used children as counters while playing it on a field! Think of this game as an action-packed ticktacktoe—with many twists and turns.

Materials
❋ Pencil
❋ Ruler
❋ Piece of poster board 12 by 12 inches square
❋ Marking pens or crayon
❋ 9 counters for each of the 2 players of two different kinds (coins, beans, buttons)

Using the pencil and ruler, draw three squares one inside the other on the poster board. The outermost square should be 9½ inches square. The middle square should be 6½ inches square. The innermost square should be 3½ inches square. Leave 1¼ inches between each square.

Draw 4 lines connecting the midpoints of the sides, as shown in the diagram below.

Draw circles at each of the corners and midpoints of the squares. Each square has 8 points, for a total of 24 points for the whole board.

Go over the pencil lines and circles with marking pens or crayons. You may also decorate your game board if you wish!

To play the game, the two players choose their nine counters—pennies vs. dimes, for example.

The two players take turns placing one counter at a time on an empty point on the game board. When all 18 counters have been placed, the players take turns moving one counter at a time along a line to the next empty point. Jumping over a counter is not allowed.

Each player tries to make a row of three along any straight line with his counters. A row of three is called a "mill." There are 16 ways to make a mill: You can make a mill along each of the four lines of each square, which equals 12 mills. And the circles you drew on the four lines connecting all three squares brings the total to 16.

A player who makes a mill removes any one of the other player's counters from the board with one exception: You may only remove a counter from the other player's existing mill if no other counter of that kind is on the board.

The mills you make are not stationary. They do not remain in their fixed positions of three in a row for the rest of the game. Rather, each counter remains in play until your opponent removes it after having formed a mill. On your next turn, you can move one of the counters from your previous mill to get into position to form another mill.

Counters that have been removed from the board are out of the game.

The losing player is the one who has only two counters left on the board or who is blocked from moving.

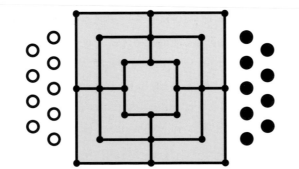

act 2, scene 3 Goodbye, Shottery.

It's a Puzzlement! What did William do for a living while he and Anne were living with his parents and they were raising a family? Again, no documentation exists. Did he work with his father? *Haply* (perhaps). Was he a schoolmaster? It's possible. What most historians agree upon is that no matter what kind of work he was engaged in, he left for London sometime after he turned 22 when the twins were barely walking. Was his marriage unhappy? Did he choose to make a living in London to recover his father's finances and status the only way he knew how—by acting and wordsmithing? Unfortunately, no diaries, scrapbooks, or letters exist to help us discover the truth.

A Life Apart. When William left his family, he said farewell not only to his loved ones, but also to a country way of life—strolling about the daisy-covered fields, taking dips in the sparkling Avon each summer, and listening closely for the approaching sounds of cattle on market day. His departure was undoubtedly filled with sorrow but also with a certain excitement at the coming journey. After all, London—the heart of English culture—was calling!

Whether or not William had a happy marriage, he obviously knew what powerful feelings love inspires. His lyrical play *Romeo and Juliet* is a testament to this. Some of the most sweet-sounding and often-repeated lines are found in the balcony scene in Act II of this play. Perhaps you will recognize some of the dialogue.

It Only Takes a Moment. Two teenagers, Romeo Montague and Juliet Capulet, meet at a ball given by Juliet's father at his home in Verona, Italy. Instantly drawn to one another, they pledge their eternal love that night in the Capulet's garden.

Romeo says to himself upon seeing Juliet by her window:

But soft, what light through yonder window breaks?

It is the East, and Juliet is the sun.

Arise, fair sun, and kill the envious moon,

Who is already sick and pale with grief

That thou, her maid, art far more fair than she.

Juliet, who has come out onto her balcony, doesn't know Romeo is near. She says to herself:

O Romeo, Romeo, wherefore art thou Romeo?

Deny thy father and refuse thy name;

Or, if thou wilt not, be but sworn my love,

And I'll no longer be a Capulet.

Upon first reading Juliet's words, we might think she is asking *where* Romeo is when she uses the word *wherefore*. But "wherefore art thou Romeo" does not mean "where are you, Romeo?" Rather, Juliet is asking, "Why are you Romeo—a Montague!—the family that my family has been fighting with for years—*my only love sprung from my only hate?* Your name has no purpose, it seems, but to interfere with our love!"

Juliet continues:

. . . What's Montague? It is nor hand nor foot,

Nor arm nor face, [nor any other part]

Belonging to a man. O, be some other name!

What's in a name? That which we call a rose

By any other word would smell as sweet;

So Romeo would, were he not Romeo call'd . . .

Alas, Romeo, by any other name, is still a Montague. So, upon hearing Juliet's words, he gives up his name. Indeed, as he said earlier, he would have gladly transformed himself into an inanimate object for her.

See how she leans her cheek upon her hand!

O that I were a glove upon that hand,

That I might touch that cheek!

Eventually, Romeo lets Juliet know that he is in her garden. And that evening, in the spotlight of the *wat'ry star's* (moon's) beams, he and Juliet make arrangements to marry.

Will Romeo and Juliet find happiness, or will their future plans unravel because of missed communications, the menacing plague, meddling parents, and miscued stars?

To learn what happens, read *Romeo and Juliet* and then you, too, will discover that:

never was a story of more woe

Than this of Juliet and her Romeo.

Night's Candles (Stars). In contrast to *Romeo and Juliet*, Shakespeare's wonderful comedy *Much Ado About Nothing* features a couple destined to be together. Throughout the play, however, determined as they are to hide their true feelings, they exchange witty *paper bullets of the brain* (insults!) instead of heartfelt lines.

The main characters in this play are Beatrice and Benedick. Beatrice, Shakespeare writes, has *little of the melancholy element in her. . . she is never sad.* Indeed, her father has heard her say that she *hath often dreamt of unhappiness, and waked herself with laughing.* And unlike Juliet, whose stars were not favorable, for Beatrice, *there was a star danc'd, and under that was [she] born.* In other words, as many in Shakespeare's audience would have believed, she was born under lucky stars; thus, her future was sealed for happiness on her birthday.

Below are several of the insulting remarks that disguise the love Beatrice and Benedick feel but don't show until the final act of the play:

Beatrice: (In response to the line, *I see, lady, the gentleman is not in your books* [good graces])

> No; and [if] he were, I would burn my study. He is sooner caught than the pestilence, and the taker runs presently mad.

In other words, he drives people crazy!

Benedick:

> If her breath were as terrible as her terminations [phrases], there were no living near her, she would infect to the north star.

A LIFE and Career in LONDON
The Nature of success

rom 1586 through 1610. William Shakespeare arrives in the capital city of London and, sometime before 1592, begins writing plays. When the plague returns to London, the theaters are closed and William turns his quill to writing sonnets and long poems. Finally, in 1594, the theaters reopen and his playwriting career takes off.

LONDON

H A M E S I S   F L V V I V S

South — Warke

16. S. Anthoines.   19. the Dutch Churche.   22. Leaden Hall.   25. S. Andrew.   27. Lion Key.   30. Alhallowes Parkins.   33. S. Katherins.
17. S. Lawrens Poultney. 20. S. Michaelis.   23. Fishmongershall.   26. S. Dunston in'   28. the Bridge.   31. Stepney.   34. S. Olofe.
18. The Exchange.   21. S. Peter.   24. S. Hellen.   de east.   29. Hackney.   32. The Tower.   35. S. Mary Ouery.

View of London as seen from the Thames

act 3, scene 2 Shakespeare arrives in London.

Hold Your Horses! As William entered London through one of the seven gates of the walled city, he undoubtedly took a walking tour. *Strolling much about* (taking the long way around) the narrow streets, past the markets, the 12 guildhalls, Inns of Court (law students' residences), and the government buildings, he had to be careful because these roads were home to about 150 thousand people as well as animals, coaches, and horses and wagons.

In the Stalls of St. Paul's. William soon learned that the hub of the city was St. Paul's Cathedral. Founded in 604 C.E., it had become not just a place to pray and hear sermons and the choir's hymns but also a gossip sharing/business meeting (some reputable, some not)/socializing center. But even more interesting were the shops and bookstalls surrounding the church's courtyard where book lovers could find the best in the printed word. There in the book market, Shakespeare could find books of popular fiction; Greek and Roman classics; Holinshed's *Chronicles of England, Scotland, and Ireland*; his beloved Roman poet Ovid's poetry, *Metamorphoses*; Geoffrey Chaucer's legends; Bible stories; novellas; and ethics

from Aesop. Some of these works Shakespeare had already read and others he would now read in order to catch up to the university-educated writers. Did William imagine then that these works would soon be joined by his own creative inventions, his poems and plays?

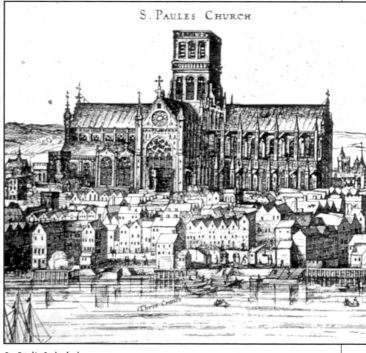

St. Paul's Cathedral

Lease means term; *date* means duration; *fair* means beauty; *untrimmed* means not beautiful; *ow'st* (ownest) means possess.

Shall **I** com**pare** thee **to** a **sum**mer's **day**? (a)
Thou **art** more **lovely and** more **temperate**: (b)
Rough **winds** do **shake** the **dar**ling **buds** of **May**, (a)
And **sum**mer's **lease** hath **all** too **short** a **date**; (b)
Some**time** too **hot** the **eye** of **heaven shines**, (c)
And **often is** his **gold** complexion **dimmed**, (d)
And **every fair** from **fair** some**time** de**clines**, (c)
By **chance** or nature's **changing course** un**trimmed**: (d)
But **thy** eternal **summer shall** not **fade**, (e)
Nor **lose** possession **of** that **fair** thou **ow'st**, (f)
Nor **shall** Death **brag** thou **wand**'rest **in** his **shade**, (e)
When **in** eternal **lines** to **time** thou **grow'st**. (f)
So **long** as **men** can **breathe** or **eyes** can **see**, (g)
So **long** lives **this**, and **this** gives **life** to **thee**. (g)

Reread the verse aloud again. Each time you read the poem, you will discover new meanings!

Vive La Difference! Shakespeare was both a poet and a playwright, composing his poems and plays with a seemingly magical ease. He wrote his sonnets in "rhymed iambic pentameter" and his plays in predominantly "unrhymed iambic pentameter," or "blank verse." Although his sonnets followed the usual pattern, he didn't allow the standard way of writing in blank verse to confine him in playwriting—he varied the style often and well so that the characters would sound even more natural.

A Quill Pen

Appropriately, Shakespeare's bust in Holy Trinity Church shows him with a quill pen in his hand. One thousand years before Shakespeare was born, the use of the quill of a goose or swan as a writing tool was introduced to Europe. The word *pen* actually comes from the Latin and Italian word for feather, *penna*, and it was with this instrument that William created his poems and plays.

Nothing can help you appreciate progress more than experiencing the way people used to do things, even if you do so for only a little while.

Materials

❋ 1 feather (Craft stores carry feathers. They also carry quill pen sets, complete with parchment paper, ink, and drying powder.)

❋ Scissors

❋ Cutting board

❋ Knife

❋ Jar of ink

❋ Paper

Adult help suggested.

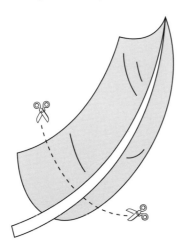

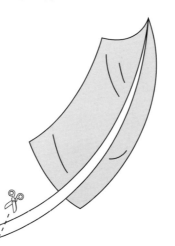

Write It Down

Centuries before the quill pen came onto the scene, the ancient Egyptians made their tool for writing by dipping reeds and hollow pieces of bamboo into ink, and the waxed tablets of the Greeks were embossed with pointed instruments made of metal. Two centuries after Shakespeare's time, real progress in writing implements was made: First, in the early 1880s, the quill point or nib was replaced with steel, most of which was supplied by Sheffield, England. Next, in 1884, came the fountain pen, an invention by Lewis E. Waterman, an American, followed four years later by the first patent for a ballpoint pen, which was issued to another American, John H. Loud. More advances in pen technology led Hungarian Lazlo Biro to make the Biro pen, which was introduced in England in 1944. Within 10 years, the ballpoint pen came to America, where today, over 2 billion are manufactured each year. Finally, in 1964, the Japanese invented the soft-tip marker.

Starting at the bottom of the quill, cut two inches of feathers along both sides of the stem with a scissors.

To create the writing nib—the point of your pen—cut the flat bottom of the stem at a sharp angle with the scissors.

Place the quill on a cutting board and, with the knife, carefully make a half-inch slit down the center of the quill, in the hollow part of the inside of the nib.

Dip your nib into the jar of ink and begin writing!

Of course, this authentic pen may be a bit frustrating to use on a regular basis. Perhaps you'd prefer to make a quasi-quill pen: Simply tape a feather to the top of your pen!

Now you are ready for the next activity—composing your own sonnet!

Compose a Sonnet

It's your turn to write a sonnet. You can devote 14 lines to anything you'd like—from the silly to the serious. With your quill in hand, think in rhyme. And remember:

1. The rhyme scheme is abab cdcd efef gg.
2. The rhythm is in iambic pentameter: Da **Da** Da **Da** Da **Da** Da **Da** Da **Da**. The *Da*s in boldface type represent the stressed syllables.

You can change the direction of your sonnet's theme after the eighth line, and then create a wonderful finale in the last two lines or "rhyming couplet" (gg).

Materials
❋ Quill pen
❋ Paper
❋ Your imagination or something audible or tangible for inspiration—a song, a picture, a memento

If you need to, you can practice writing in iambic pentameter and rhyme by filling in the following sonnet about Halloween. Each line represents a missing syllable.

1—On Halloween, I'll wear __ __ white sheet

2—And trick or treat away the whole night long.

3—Those chocolate __ __ surely can't be beat.

4—Oh, what a thrill I feel with each ding-dong!

5—I have a lot of neighbors, which is great,

6—And filling up __ bag's my only job.

7—Sometimes if I am __ I have to wait

8—As I push through the __ __ __ __ mob.

9—A treat it is to think I'll eat them __.

10—But first I have to fill my bag with more,

11—Beneath the __ __ sky and __ __ moon,

12—As I walk far away from my front door.

13—I wonder who's in charge __ __ __ __?

14—A ghost I am, but __ __ just the same.

Here are a few suggestions to fill in the blanks:

line 1: an old; a big

line 3: candies; kisses

line 6: my; this

line 7: late; slow

line 8: hungry; costumed; scary-looking

line 9: soon

line 11: first blank: starless; pitch black; darkened;
second blank: howling; chilly

line 13: and who's to blame; I want his (her) name

line 14: fearful; frightened

And here's a complete sonnet:

On Halloween, I'll wear an old white sheet
And trick or treat away the whole night long.
Those chocolate candies surely can't be beat.
Oh, what a thrill I feel with each ding-dong!

I have a lot of neighbors, which is great,
And filling up my bag's my only job.

Sometimes if I am slow I have to wait
As I push through the hungry, costumed mob.
A treat it is to think I'll eat them soon.
But first I have to fill my bag with more,
Beneath the starless sky and howling moon,
As I walk far away from my front door.
I wonder who's in charge and who's to blame?
A ghost I am, but frightened just the same.

Before writing your own sonnet, perhaps you'd
like to complete a sonnet that begins like Shakespeare's Sonnet number 18:

Shall I compare thee to a starry night?
Thou hast more radiance and warming glow.
The distance of the stars, their soaring height,
Make people feel so very small below.

When you've finished this one, it's time to begin
your own! Sonnets may be a bit tricky at first, but
don't give up. If a complete sonnet is a bit too difficult, why not try to write down two lines that rhyme.
Write just a few more rhyming lines and you'll have a
sonnet in no time!

act 3, scene 5 The theaters reopen!

Shakespeare Is in Good Company. When the playhouses reopened in 1594, James Burbage, the owner of The Theatre, formed a new acting company. The lead actor was his son, Richard. Joining Richard were probably these six men who had previously been players with Lord Strange's Men: Richard Cowley, John Heminges, Augustine Phillips, George Bryan, Thomas Pope, and William Kempe.

Shakespeare in good company

And what 30-year-old actor and poet (playwright) joined the group as a partner (sharer)? William Shakespeare! As a sharer, William helped pay the company's production expenses, and in return, he received a portion of the profits. Now, under the patronage of Henry Carey, the Lord Chamberlain of England, William and his fellow actors would from that day forward be known as the Lord Chamberlain's Men. Financially, the Chamberlain's Men did extremely well, and William became their star poet. James Burbage's The Theatre, north of London, in Shoreditch, was their home in the summer. And during the rest of the year, performances were held at the Cross Keys Inn—that is, until 1596, when the authorities banned plays within the city limits.

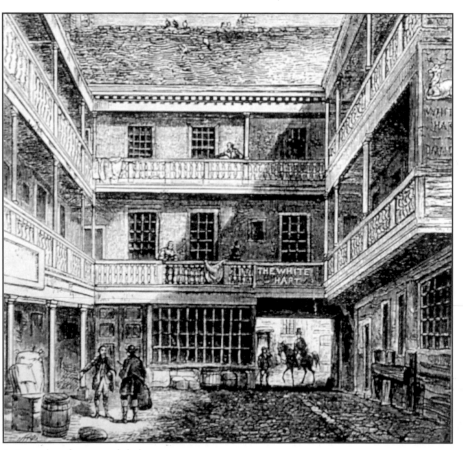

An inn yard—a forerunner of playhouses

act 3, scene 6 Hamnet Shakespeare dies.

Good Night, Sweet Prince. Professionally, William was doing very well, but *life's uncertain voyage* ran into rough seas in 1596. On August 11, 1596, William and Anne Shakespeare's son, Hamnet, was laid to rest. Only 11 years old, his life had been as *swift as a shadow* and as *brief as the lightning*. Was it an ill-ness? An accident? We're not sure. Though there is no evidence that William was in Stratford to bid farewell to his son, we can presume he was. And we can further assume that he and his family held Hamnet's *shining morning face* affectionately in their hearts for the rest of their lives.

Hamnet Shakespeare's burial record

аст 3, scene 7 The Burbage brothers find a new home for the Lord Chamberlain's Men.

The Globe

All's Well That Ends Well. By 1596, James Burbage was in trouble. The Theatre had been built on leased land, and his 21-year lease would soon expire. He tried to negotiate with the landlord for a renewal of their contract, but he and the owner could not reach a new agreement. Then, Burbage died in January 1597, so it was left up to his son, Cuthbert Burbage, who inherited The Theatre, to save it. Unfortunately, Cuthbert's attempts at negotiating failed as well.

When Cuthbert Burbage and his brother, Richard, the lead actor of the Lord Chamberlain's Men, learned that their landlord was planning to pull down The Theatre to use the timber for another purpose, they had to hurry and devise a plan. And in December 1598, their scheme went into action: A hired carpenter, a dozen or so workmen, the Burbages, and their friend dismantled The Theatre in Shoreditch. Then they transported the oak timbers across the Thames River to another area free from city authorities called Southwark. Home to the city's prisons, hospitals, and gambling establishments, this was where they would rebuild their playhouse. To pay for the new lease for the land and construction of the new theater, all the Burbages needed now was money. They had half of the required sum, but where would they get the rest?

Enter, Players. Within eight months, thanks to the partners' financial support, a new playhouse was built from the timbers of the old theater. They called their new home The Globe. Now, as co-owners of The Globe—there was no building rent to pay!—the Lord Chamberlain's Men earned an even greater portion of the box-office success of the company.

The Chamberlain's Men were so successful that Shakespeare was able to invest his share of the profits in properties back home, just as his father had done before him. In 1597, he purchased New Place, the second-largest house in town. And three years after The Globe opened, he was able to buy a cottage and some land in Stratford. But that wasn't all: Financial success meant that he could afford to renew his father's application for a coat of arms, which was granted. Finally, the Shakespeares were officially gentlemen.

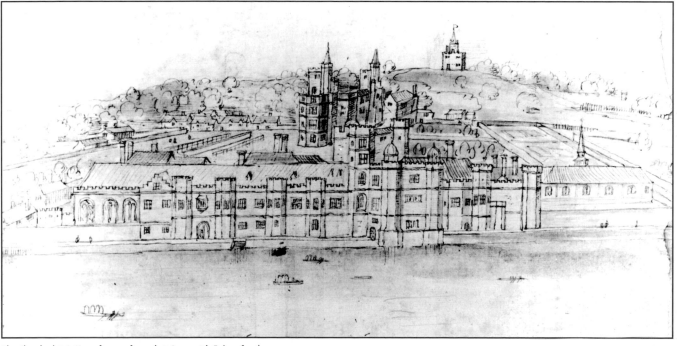

The Chamberlain's Men often performed at Greenwich Palace for the queen.

Design a Coat of Arms

The motto reads: *Non sanz droict*, which means "not without right."

When John Shakespeare was doing well financially and was an esteemed member of the town council, he began his application to obtain a coat of arms with an official called the Garter King of Arms. This application was made with the Heralds College, which had been established in 1483. A coat of arms was an honor because it meant that a person had gained membership into the gentry class.

Unfortunately, the process of applying was expensive and, because of money problems, John Shakespeare was unable to follow through with his application. Twenty-eight years later, in 1596, when William was doing well in the theater, he applied for a coat of arms in his father's name and it was granted. Finally, and legally in the eyes of society, John Shakespeare was a gentleman. And his entire family had every reason to feel proud of that!

William loved puns. The design of the Shakespeare coat of arms shows just how clever he was. It is of a falcon holding—or perhaps even shaking—a spear. Spear—Shakespeare! In the world of heraldry, this punning is called *canting*.

A coat of arms is an artistic representation of things such as "genealogy," or ancestry, and honors. The coat of arms began in medieval times with the use of knights' armor. Their shields, as well as the garments they wore over their armor, called "surcoats," were decorated with various symbols and colors so they could identify one another. This symbolic language is called "heraldry." Today, companies, universities, states, countries, and commonwealths have coats of arms and other similarly symbolic graphic images such as emblems, seals, and flags.

The main parts of a coat of arms are the crest, wreath (or torse), helmet, mantling, shield, bend, charge, supporters, scroll, and motto. The basic design of a coat of arms is based upon those items that a medieval knight (soldier) wore or carried in battle—his shield, helmet, mantle, wreath, and crest.

Materials

❋ Sketching paper
❋ Pencil
❋ Poster board
❋ Crayons and marking pens
❋ Tape or glue

Optional: access to a color photocopy machine
Decide how you will design your personal coat of arms. Do you have a favorite sport? If so, then you might want to include a baseball, a football, a tennis racket, or ice skates in your design. Do you love ballet? Then how about decorating it with ballet slippers? Or do what William Shakespeare did and create something that plays with your name. The artistic symbols that you choose as decoration for your coat of arms are called "charges."

Pick a shape for your shield. You may also choose to divide the surface of your shield with lines called "partitions." Choose colors to decorate your coat of arms.

TENNIS, ANYONE?

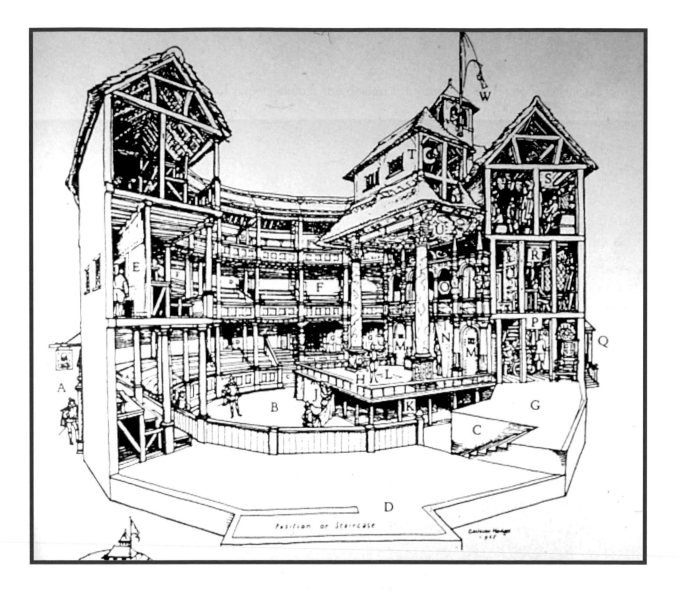

A Main entrance
B The yard
C Entrances to lowest gallery
D Position of entrances to staircase and upper galleries
E Corridor serving the different sections of the middle gallery
F Middle gallery ("twopenny rooms")

G Position of "gentlemen's rooms" or "lords' rooms"
H The stage
J The hanging being put up round the stage
K The "hell" under the stage
L The stage trap leading down to the hell
M Stage doors

N Curtained "place behind the stage"
O Gallery above the stage, used as required sometimes by musicians, sometimes by spectators, and often as part of the play.
P Backstage area (the tiring-house)
Q Tiring-house door

R Dressing rooms
S Wardrobe and storage
T The hut housing the machine for lowering enthroned gods, etc. to the stage
U "The heavens"
W Hoisting the playhouse flag

A cross section of The Globe Theater

acт 3, scene 8 A day at the theater.

Get Me to The Globe on Time. To attend a play at The Globe or at one of the other theaters on Bankside in Southwark, one had to cross the Thames River either by walking over London Bridge or by taking a boat. One 16th-century Swiss traveler, Thomas Platter, described his experience:

> It is customary to cross the water or travel up and down the town . . . by attractive pleasure craft, for a number of tiny streets lead to the Thames from both ends of the town; the boatmen wait there in great crowds, each one eager to be the first to catch one, for all are free to choose the ship they find most attractive and pleasing, while every boatman has the privilege on arrival of placing his ship to best advantage for people to step into. . . .

Just nine months after The Theatre had been dismantled and rebuilt, the Lord Chamberlain's Men were home again. Thomas Platter was there too:

> On 21 September after dinner, at about 2 o'clock, I and my party crossed the water . . . [where] we saw the tragedy of the first Emperor Julius Caesar, very pleasantly performed, with approximately fifteen characters . . .

After every play—even after sad stories—a jig was performed because the performers didn't want the audience to go home unhappy. As Thomas Platter wrote, "...they danced together admirably and exceedingly gracefully, according to their custom, two in each group dressed in men's and two in women's apparel." (This last bit of news was one of the reasons the Puritans had such a problem with actors!)

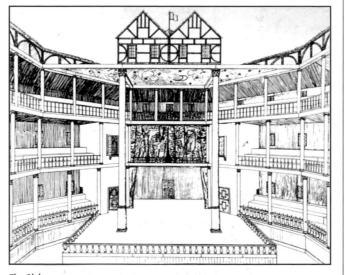

The Globe stage

QUESTIONS AND ANSWERS ABOUT THE THEATER IN SHAKESPEARE'S DAY:

What was the stage like?

The stage itself was four to five feet high and about 940 square feet in size, and surrounded by a railing. The ceiling above the stage, which was supported by two columns, was painted with the sun, moon, stars, and Zodiac signs. The columns themselves were made of wood and were perhaps painted to look like marble. Instead of relying on scenery to indicate the time of day, the audience was told what time it was with props and words called "scene painting." For example, the sight of a torch to light the way or the mention of a morning lark instructed the audience that it was night or day. In addition, fake heads, makeup, fireworks—for lightning—swords, and vials for poison *quicken*[ed] (animated) the scenes of the plays. Finally, the company had extravagant properties to dress the stage—thrones, caves, lion's skins, tables, trees, draperies, tapestries, and so much more.

There are only a few female characters in Shakespeare's plays. Why?

Only boys and men were allowed to act on the stage. Women were not allowed to perform because it was thought improper for them to take such a role in society. That is why there are few female roles—*Julius Caesar* has just two!—and romantic scenes are more verbal than physical.

Beginning at about the age of 10, boys apprenticed to players in the company. This meant that the young men were fed and housed and trained to act, sing, and dance. When the boys grew up, they could join the company of 20 to 30 men as "sharers," leading actors as well as stockholders, or become hired workers as wardrobe men, bookkeepers, ticket takers (gatherers), stagehands, musicians, or walk-on players. Of course, not all actors began by apprenticing. Some, like William Shakespeare, became actors as adults.

How did the actors prepare for a play?

A scribe prepared "fair copies" from the writer's original manuscripts called "foul papers." The term *foul papers* was created because the original versions were not always in good condition and they were difficult to read because they were filled with crossouts and markings. Each player was given his part, which included his lines, his cues, and instructions for entering and exiting the stage. Amazingly, the actors, who memorized a new part in about two weeks, kept hundreds of lines of dialogue from over 30 different plays in their heads. And if they ever missed their cue, a prompter was just off stage to assist.

What were the rules governing who could perform which plays?

The Lord Chamberlain's Men bought and performed not only William's plays but also other poets' plays. Once a company bought a play, it could not be performed by any other company unless it was sold to them or to a publisher. If a company owned a successful play, for which it had paid the playwright five to eight pounds (after 1600, the price rose to 10 to 12 pounds), that company would only part with it if it needed the money.

Shakespeare's first play to be published was *Titus Andronicus*, in 1594. Within a few years, *Romeo and Juliet*, *Henry IV, Part I*, *Richard II*, and *Richard III* were published. Soon, the name Shakespeare was a *household word*.

What were the stages between receiving and performing a new play? And what was rehearsal like?

In three weeks, a new play was accepted (by the acting company and the queen's censor, the Master of the Revels), the costumes and props were gathered, and the actors learned their lines. The final step before the first performance was rehearsal.

Rehearsal on the day of that first performance (and sometimes a play only had one performance!) lasted from morning until around noon. The players would block their movements—reviewing where they would stand on the stage and how and when they would enter and exit through the doors at the back of the stage. Actors playing ghosts and devils practiced their entrances and exits through the trap door to an area below the stage called "hell." Others perfected being lowered onto the stage from a trap door in what was called "the heavens" via heavy machinery and ropes located in the hut above the stage.

Musicians gathered their instruments—bandores, lutes, citterns, sackbuts (similar to trombones), flutes, pipes, horns, trumpets, and drums—and rehearsed their drum rolls for the perfect clap of thunder or rousing sounds of battle. And, when necessary, cannon fire would be used to great effect.

The Play's the Thing

Of the city's 200,000–250,000 people, approximately 10 percent saw a play every week. Some plays ran for only one or two performances, but a successful play could have a much longer run. A few popular plays, such as those written by Shakespeare, were revived years after their premieres.

Sound Effects

When writer/actor William Shakespeare appeared on the scene, he was called a *Johannes fac totum* (jack-of-all-trades) by Robert Greene. More than 300 years later, a modern form of entertainment called talking pictures was invented, and another jack-of-all-trades—Jack Foley—made history as well when he invented sound effects. Today, sound-effects engineers are called, appropriately, foley artists! Look for them the next time you watch the credits scroll after a movie. In Shakespeare's day, theatrical sound effects were created simply. For instance, the drum roll could signal Caesar's parade or suggest distant thunder. A shot of cannon fire could indicate the start of battle. Today, sound directors can buy recordings of sound effects or tape their own. You can make—and record!—your own sound effects, too. Try these for starters.

Materials

* Baking sheet, large
* Metal wastebasket, empty
* Pair of shoes
* Pots and pans

Optional: tape recorder

To make a thunderstorm: Shake a large baking sheet.

To make an echo: Hold an empty metal wastebasket to the side of and a little bit away from your mouth and talk partly into it, partly away from it. This way, your voice is half way in the wastebasket and half way outside the wastebasket (you'll also be able to hear yourself better).

To make footsteps: Put one hand inside one shoe and your other hand inside the other shoe. With your hands, walk the shoes across the floor. Begin by tapping the heel down first and then the toe with one shoe, and then the heel and then the toe with the other.

To make a crashing sound: Drop several pots and pans onto a floor. Be sure to warn people ahead of time!

If a tape recorder is available, record your sound effects and play them back.

aCT 3, scene 9 It's show time!

A Fanfare! As the hour for the performance drew near, a colorful flag was raised and the fanfare from a trumpeter announced this fact from the tower atop the theater. This was the routine six days a week, unless bad weather prevented the show from going on. A white flag symbolized a comedy. The comedies are lighthearted tales of mistaken identities, false pride, and love. They are not purely fun, however, because a few of these plays also feature mean-spirited characters who try to ruin the main characters' happiness. In the end, however, these stories conclude joyfully. *Much Ado About Nothing* is one of these comedies. A black flag meant a tragedy was on the program that day. The tragedies are stories about noble people who, because of their fate, their own flaws, or both, make decisions that lead to their ruin. *Romeo and Juliet* and *Hamlet* are two of Shakespeare's tragedies. A red flag signified a historical play—usually the story of an English monarch. These plays are about power struggles in English history. *Richard III* and *Henry V* are two of the history plays.

Whether tragedy, history, or comedy, Shakespeare's plays are filled with memorable characters, proverbs, jokes, and puns. Today, five of Shakespeare's 38 plays are called romances. But in Shakespeare's day, this category did not exist. Thus, before a performance, only one of three flags was required. Today, if we were to advertise a romance play, we would have to hoist a flag of a completely different color.

Standing Room Only. The audience was filing inside. *Anon* (soon), 3,000 people—laborers, servants, apprentices, merchants, military officers, law students, nobles, and tourists—would fill the theater.

The wealthy were dressed in the fashionable clothes of the day, creating quite a spectacle. Women's skirts were formed into cone shapes with the help of *farthingales* (stiffened hoops) or a *bum roll* (a padded roll worn around the hips—it made the skirt flare out and the woman's waist appear small). Stockings were hand-knitted and made of silk; on their hands were gloves, often embroidered with gold and silver thread; around their necks they wore a *ruff* (a large, round pleated collar); and, to finish the look, they wore a hat or intricate hairstyle. Men were dressed in knitted stockings, *trunk hose* (short, full pants reaching about halfway down the thigh), quilted waistcoats covered with doublets made with removable sleeves, silk shirts, ruff collars, embroidered capes or cloaks, and hats.

The *groundlings* (those who would stand around the stage on ground level) had paid their penny admission into a box. Those who could afford another penny walked upstairs to sit on one of the benches in the first gallery. For a third penny and a better view, a spectator could sit in one of the seats in the two top galleries. Finally, for a sixpence—or six pennies or half a shilling—a playgoer could sit in one of the private rooms near the stage.

Hungry for More than Words, Words, Words? William's plays, as all others at that time, consisted of five acts and lasted two to three hours. For spectators who arrived on an empty stomach, vendors were on hand to provide snacks of fruit, nuts, and gingerbread. Water and beer were available as well. Sometimes, food was not just used for eating:

If members of the audience didn't like a particular performance, they booed, walked out—or threw food! More often, however, they were pleased with what they saw and heard and applauded appreciatively.

When the show was over, perhaps William would be invited for supper at one of the inns in town. Surely he must have accepted the invitation to *come and crush a cup of wine* (have a drink) and to join a lively conversation—and perhaps a dish of pudding—before returning to the task of finishing his latest manuscript.

Such was the *workyday* (everyday) life of an acting company. They had Sundays off, but in addition to productions at the Globe, they gave evening performances for royalty, nobles, and students. If you think about everything William had to do—involving himself in the many details of putting on six different plays a week, writing two splendid plays every year, and traveling back and forth from London to Stratford to visit his family—a picture of his eventful life emerges.

A Goblet for a Prop

As a glove-maker, William's father may have decorated the gauntlets of gloves with embossed ornaments called goblets. That's one kind of goblet. The other kind is the more commonly known drinking vessel, which you can make as a prop. Or, make a set of these and fill them with candy for a wonderful party favor!

Materials

✻ Aluminum foil or foil wrapping paper

✻ Scissors

✻ Plastic cup, 4 inches tall

✻ Double-sided tape

Optional: Different colors of foil, smaller cup, candy wrappers

Cut a piece of foil 12 inches across by 24 inches long.

Using the plastic cup as a mold, place the cup at one corner of the foil, aligning the top of the cup with the edge of the foil, and then loosely wrap the foil around and around the plastic cup. Pinch the foil at the bottom of the cup to create a stem.

Remove the cup.

Tape the two loose ends of the foil to itself, inside the goblet and outside too.

Pinch the goblet to create the stem of the goblet. Leave enough foil to create a base.

Flatten the remaining foil into a base.

Optional: Wrap foil around the stem and base of the goblet in a different color than you used for the top, or line the inside of the goblet with a contrasting color! Also, if you want to make a smaller goblet, use half or three-quarters the amount of foil and a smaller cup. If you want to make miniature goblets, take candy wrappers and, using your fingers as a guide, create the goblet as described above.

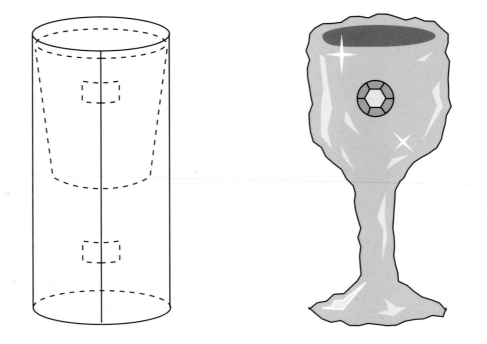

ACT 3, SCENE 10   Queen Elizabeth I dies.

Intrigue Fit for a Shakespearean Play. On February 6, 1601, Shakespeare and his company became unwittingly involved in a plot to overthrow the queen. Here's how the story unfolded.

Robert Devereux, the Earl of Essex, once a favorite of Elizabeth's, had only one thought by 1601—to overthrow the queen. Why? Because she had had him arrested for political reasons and, after his release, he had been stripped of his titles. As part of the plan, he and his men—the Earl of Southampton, Shakespeare's former patron, was among them—decided that before they could attempt such a dangerous mission, they should rally the citizens behind them. To accomplish this, some of the earl's supporters arranged for the Lord Chamberlain's Men to perform *Richard II* the next day at the Globe—the day before the planned uprising. They chose this particular play because it was about the removal of a weak king.

Regrettably for them, this performance did nothing to put Londoners in a rebellious mood. And, thus, on February 8 the earl and his men failed terri-

Robert Devereux, the Earl of Essex

bly. For their part, the Lord Chamberlain's Men had a bit of explaining to do. Augustine Phillips, one of the members of the company, was one of those who testified. Although we don't know much else about what happened, the company was cleared of any suspicion. Yes, they had accepted money to perform this play, but, thankfully, they had been unaware of the reason for that special request.

Two weeks later, on February 24, the night before the Earl of Essex's execution, the Lord Chamberlain's Men performed for the queen. And what happened to the Earl of Southampton? His death sentence was reduced to life imprisonment in the Tower of London. But he did not stay there long because in 1603, the new king, James I, set the accused man free and actually made him a "courtier"—a servant at the royal court!

The Lord Chamberlain's Men entertain the queen.

A New Era. Elizabeth I died in 1603. During her reign of 45 years, literature and theater blossomed in England. Her favorite acting company, the Lord Chamberlain's Men, would now perform under the patronage of her distant cousin—the new king—James VI of Scotland. James I, as he was called in England, took on the responsibility of the Lord Chamberlain's Men and renamed them the King's Men. This new era is called the Jacobean period because the Latin word for James is *Jacobus*.

During Shakespeare's lifetime, his company performed four times as much for the king as it had for the queen, providing them with much respect and even more income! But just two years before the queen died, William must have wondered for a moment if he and his company would ever work again. . . .

act 3, scene 11 William nears the end of his career in London.

He'd Grown Accustomed to the Place. The morning songbirds did not awaken William because he'd been up all night working on his latest script, *Coriolanus*. Writing two plays a year, this latest endeavor brought the number of his plays up to 33. But today, number 32, *Pericles*, was premiering.

Jumping up from his desk, he gathered his papers and walked out the door for rehearsal, which would occupy his entire morning. As William approached the round-looking theater, he realized that he never tired of seeing it. Although he'd certainly grown accustomed to it, the joy and magic it held for him remained fresh.

The Globe, he knew, was actually a polygon that had been designed in the style of the ancient Greek and Roman amphitheaters. As he approached it, he recalled the many hours of preparation that had occupied his company's time throughout the years.

William hoped that only good luck would bless this newest production. For instance, *Macbeth*, which had premiered just two years ago, had not had a pleasant opening night because the boy who was supposed to play Lady Macbeth suddenly died.

It's Play Time Again! *Macbeth* is a play about how a once honest and victorious Scottish army commander becomes obsessed with being king and loses everything, including his life, because of it. As the audience soon learns, there are three forces at work that will eventually ruin him: First, Macbeth hears predictions from the *midnight hags* (witches) that he will someday be king of Scotland. Second, his wife, Lady Macbeth, nags him to do whatever is necessary to become the ruler, even if it means murder. And third, he begins, in the name of ambition, to cast off his tags (badges) of honor, morality, and ethics, which he once wore with pride.

That Old Black Magic. Three conniving witches stir up trouble for Macbeth, the man who would be king. As our scene opens, their spell is uttered above the threatening sounds of thunder (drum roll, please):

> Round about the cauldron go;
> In the poisoned entrails throw . . .
> Double, double, toil and trouble;
> Fire burn, and cauldron bubble.
> Fillet of a fenny snake,
> In the cauldron boil and bake;
> Eye of newt and toe of frog,
> Wool of bat and tongue of dog . . .
> For a charm of powerful trouble,
> Like a hell-broth boil and bubble.
> Double, double toil and trouble;
> Fire burn, and cauldron bubble.

Three witches

At first, the thought of committing murder makes Macbeth's hair stand on end. But soon, with his wife's prodding, he dismisses this disgust and commits the first of several horrible acts—he kills Duncan, the King of Scotland. Macbeth's once-noble compass is now *tempest-tossed* and it is just a question of time when all will be *lost* (destroyed).

Playing with History. William was a successful playwright in his day because he could move a story full of people along so entertainingly. His stories have had lasting impact because he was able to reveal the many sides of people as they struggled with their problems. Whether the story was about aristocrats, teenagers, soldiers, or ghosts of kings, it was their human qualities of jealousy, hatred, love, desire, and ambition that touched, and still affect, our hearts and minds.

Of course, the audience was not always seeing history as it actually happened. First of all, the most widely read historical text of Shakespeare's day, Holinshed's *Chronicles of England, Scotland, and Ireland*, was not entirely accurate. Some of the articles in that book often repeated legend, not fact. Secondly, the queen's censor, known as the Master of the Revels, made sure that there was nothing politically or religiously improper in the plays. This meant that if a member of the monarch's family had done something wrong or immoral, William had to rewrite the past. Also, for creative reasons, he often played with history's dates and characters. For example, the events that transpire in another of Shakespeare's plays, *Antony and Cleopatra*, cover 10 years in actual history. But on the stage, William reduced this time period to 12 days. Why? Because the creation of compelling and dramatic theater came first!

Macbeth is another good example of how Shakespeare played with history. In reality, the historical Macbeth (1005–1057 C.E.) started a civil war and became king after he killed Duncan, the King of Scotland, in battle in 1040. Also, Macbeth's reign was peaceful and lasted for 17 years. Thankfully, for the sake of great theater, William had an imagination!

Create a Slashed-Shirt Costume

The costumes of the actors who played noble people were dazzling. Sometimes servants received these clothes as gifts from their "noble" employers and then sold them to the companies. These poorer people had to sell the clothes because it was unlawful for anyone to wear clothing worn by a higher-ranking person. Another source for the costuming was the patron who supported the company.

Costumes did not usually represent what people wore during the period in history in which the play took place. But this didn't seem to matter to the audience. It was only important that the clothes represent the position that a character had in society. Occasionally, one costume cost as much or more than the manuscript itself!

These costumes were kept in the *tiring room* (attiring or dressing room), which was hidden behind curtains at the back of the stage. The yellow silk and velvet gowns, scarlet cloaks with gold buttons, ginger-colored doublets, and the *motley* (multicolored) outfits added greatly to the production.

This activity presents a type of clothing style from the 1400s called "slashing," which gave the clothes a colorful, layered look.

Materials
❀ 2 long T-shirts in bold, contrasting colors
❀ Scissors
❀ 1 rope for a belt
❀ 1 pair of colored tights
Adult help suggested.

Decide which T-shirt you will wear underneath the other one.

For long-sleeved T-shirts: Slash the sleeves of the top T-shirt by cutting a few rows of three-inch-long vertical slits from just below the shoulder seam to the bottom of the sleeve. Do not cut into the hem of the sleeve. Space each slit about one inch apart.

Important Rules

1. Safety is most important. It is something you plan and it is the most important consideration of all.

2. Safe Distance: Keeping a safe distance is vital. Stand far enough apart so that 12 inches of space exist between the point of your fully extended sword and the navel of your opponent at all times.

3. Placement: Never let your sword cross your opponent's face or body. Except for the "thrust," a movement aimed at the opponent's navel, the point is otherwise never aimed at the other child. There should be no waving of the sword. Think of the area around your opponent's body as having an invisible force field. Your movements are always around, not toward, the other person.

4. Every move is planned in advance and you and your opponent are working together—your sword is not moving faster than your opponent's. There are no surprises.

5. Focus: Always keep in mind that what you are doing is playing, not fighting. It only gives the illusion of a fight.

6. Practice: Practice over and over again until you can skillfully move in a designed way safely.

To make the guard, roll the sheet of newspaper into the shape of a tube. Cut several inches off one end so that the paper guard will be 6 inches long. Flatten it and cut a hole in the middle of it. The hole should be large enough for the cardboard wrapping-paper tube to fit through it. Slip the tube through the hole until about seven inches of the tube is left. This seven inches will be the handle of the sword.

Tape the guard to the cardboard tube securely.

Twist the ends of the guard slightly. Tape the ends of the newspaper to bind the edges.

Cover and decorate the blade of your sword (the cardboard tube) and the guard by wrapping gold, silver, or any other color of crepe paper around it.

Wrap the crepe paper around and around the blade and the guard many times until it is one unit with no sharp edges. Tape the crepe paper to the tube and guard as you wind it around to prevent it from unraveling. Don't wrap the guard and blade separately. Rather, wrap the crepe paper around one side of the guard and then cross it over to the other side, thereby anchoring it even further to the blade portion of the sword. When you are finished wrapping, secure the crepe paper with tape at the ends.

Push two styrofoam balls into each end of the tube, letting them stick out a bit. Alternatively, if you can't find styrofoam balls, wad up some newspaper or aluminum foil into a ball and use this for the "tip" of the sword and to reinforce the handle.

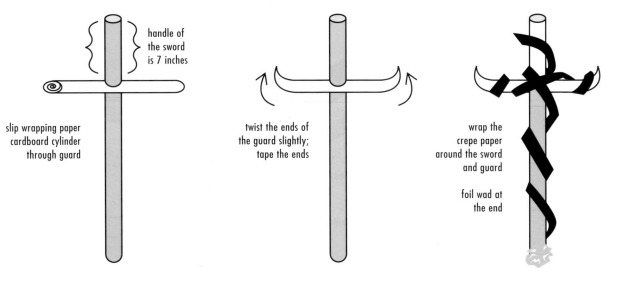

handle of the sword is 7 inches

slip wrapping paper cardboard cylinder through guard

twist the ends of the guard slightly; tape the ends

wrap the crepe paper around the sword and guard

foil wad at the end

Stage a Sword Fight

For theatrical productions, actors had to know not only how to speak the lines effectively but also how to dance, do stunts, and handle props. In particular, sword fights had to be practiced over and over again if they were going to be convincing to the audience members sitting and standing inches away from the stage.

Shakespeare used the power of his pen to write dramatic dueling scenes, which often led to tragic consequences for a play's characters. In *Romeo and Juliet*, Juliet's cousin, Tybalt, and Romeo's best friend, Mercutio, engage in a sword fight. Because Romeo has just secretly married Tybalt's cousin, Juliet, he desires nothing but peace between himself and his new cousin. So, in trying to help put a stop to the fight, he and another friend, Benvolio, try to separate Tybalt and Mercutio by coming between them. In so doing, Romeo interferes and gives Tybalt a chance to deliver a fatal thrust to Mercutio. Moments before Mercutio dies, he says, *A plague o'* [on] *both your houses!* Having read about the plague, you understand the devastation of that curse.

Never thrust. Don't aim the point of your sword at, or even near, your opponent's body.

HERE ARE SOME INSTRUCTIONS FOR STAGING YOUR OWN SWORD FIGHT:

Position
Stand facing your opponent with your feet wide apart, your right foot forward and turned out slightly, and your left back foot turned out to a 45-degree angle (see diagram). Bend your knees slightly.

The High-Low-High Sequence
(Note: All directions for sword fighting are given for a right-handed person.)

To begin: Standing a safe distance from each other, hold the sword in your right hand and point it to your left and to the side of your opponent's body at about waist height.

Both opponents: Raise your right arm, moving it in a semicircular, clockwise motion around and up and over the head toward the center line, letting your swords meet in what's called the "top hat" position. The two swords meet above your heads and cross in the middle. Let them touch slightly. Now, lower your right arm to your left again, guiding the sword away (stay away from your opponent's face and body) in a semicircular, counterclockwise motion, and bring the swords together in the low position at the feet (see diagram). The point of each sword should be pointing at your opponent's foot in the low position. As you raise and lower your arm with the sword, think of yourself tracing and retracing the outline of a half moon. From this low position, sweep up in a semicircle to the top hat position once more. Repeat this sequence as many times as you like.

Add Footwork
(Note: When you advance forward, beginning with your right foot, you step "heel then toe." When you retreat, beginning with your left foot, you step "toe then heel." Whenever one person advances, the other retreats, which ensures that there will be a safe distance between the two at all times.)

With your swords in high position, you and your opponent will sweep your swords in that semicircular motion to the low position. Just as you both reach that low position, right before the blades touch, your opponent steps back as you step forward. That safe distance spoken of earlier is maintained at all times.

Then, without any stepping, you and your opponent guide your blades back up into the high position using that semicircular motion once again.

From this high position, you and your opponent again sweep your swords in that semicircular motion to the low position. This time, though, just as you both reach that low position, right before the blades touch, you step back as your opponent steps forward. Again, that safe distance spoken of earlier is maintained at all times. You can repeat this sequence as many times as you like.

Thrust and Lunge Movement
From the low position, your sword and your opponent's sword separate, and you each move your swords to the right. Then, you extend your sword toward your opponent's navel (this movement is called a thrust). Even with the extension of your sword, 12 inches of space still exist between you and your opponent because, at the same time that your sword is extended, your opponent steps back. Then, you step forward (lunge), bending your right knee deeply. Then, in defense, your opponent's sword is lifted over your heads in a counterclockwise motion and the middle of the blade is lowered to meet your sword, gently guiding it to the right. Your opponent's move is a defensive move called "a universal parry."

Then, you and your opponent slowly guide your swords over your heads using the semicircular motion again. Your swords are now pointing to your left and away from your opponent's body at about waist height, which is the starting position.

You can repeat this sequence of moves, this time allowing your opponent to be the one who lunges and thrusts.

Back to the High-Low-High Sequence—and Then the "Kill"
Repeat the High-Low-High sequence without moving forward or backward.

To end the sword fight—called "the kill"—begin from the high position. Let the swords meet in the low position once more, but this time allow the swords to follow through their arc and disengage. You then go back to a top hat position at which point your opponent—from the right—lifts the point of his sword from his shoulder over his head in a counterclockwise direction to your right side. With the sword now on your side—and with the edge, never the point—your opponent leans forward to tap your right side.

Then your opponent pulls his blade back and establishes distance before you—with your face high and away from your opponent's blade—lower yourself to the floor gently in defeat, without letting your knees hit the floor hard and without hitting your opponent with your sword.

Produce a Scene from Julius Caesar

Reader's Tip

You may want to read the entire play of *Julius Caesar* and become familiar with the plot and the characters. The New Folger Library edition of each of Shakespeare's plays summarizes every scene of each of the five acts for you. You can read through these before deciding which scene to act out.

In nine easy steps, using the props you have made and the staged sword fight techniques you have learned, you can bring a scene from *Julius Caesar* to life! Later, if you see this part of the play performed by professionals, you will appreciate it even more.

Julius Caesar is set in Rome. The action begins on February 15, the day of the Feast of Lupercal, a Roman festival. A fortune-teller is warning Roman ruler Julius Caesar to *beware the ides* (the 15th) *of March*. While he dismisses the fortune-teller as just a dreamer, the men who oppose Caesar because of his ambition to be king discuss killing him.

1. Choose a Scene. The six scenes summarized below are suggestions to get you started. Keep in mind that many vocabulary words from Shakespeare's time are no longer in use. For instance, the word *schedule*, which you know to mean "timetable," means "document" in *Julius Caesar*. The play should define these unfamiliar terms somewhere on the same page.

a. Act 1, Scene 1: This is a short street scene that takes place in Rome. Caesar has just returned home in triumph after having defeated his rival, Pompey. The people have taken the day off from work to celebrate. There are four speaking roles, a noisy group of citizens, and one especially impassioned speech. There is also some fun with puns.

b. Act 1, Scene 3: This is a fairly short scene with four roles and the chance to try visual and sound effects. In this scene, which opens with thunder and lightning, the conspiracy against Caesar builds, and the dialogue is strong and vivid.

c. Act 2, Scene 1: This is a tender husband-and-wife scene (Brutus and Portia) that takes place in the garden. It includes roles for the seven of eight conspirators and a young servant. In this scene, Brutus is drawn into the conspiracy against Caesar.

d. Act 2, Scene 2: This scene is set in Caesar's palace. It is the 15th of March—the day that the fortune-teller warned Caesar about when he said, *beware the ides of March*. Caesar's wife, Calpurnia, has had a terrifying nightmare and convinces her husband that it is not safe for him to leave home. Then, Decius, one of the conspirators, arrives and reinterprets Calpurnia's nightmare. Thus, Caesar changes his mind and goes to the Capitol, which will be the scene of his death.

e. Act 3, Scene 1: This scene takes place in the Capitol in Rome. It is an action scene in which the conspirators—even the *gentle* (noble) Brutus—assassinate Caesar. Mark Antony, in barely controlled grief, confronts the conspirators.

f. Act 3, Scene 2: This scene takes place outdoors in the streets. A crowd of shocked citizens gathers to hear Brutus's explanation of why Caesar was murdered. His speech includes the memorable line *not that I loved Caesar less, but that I loved Rome more*. Mark Antony gives the real funeral oration that begins *Friends, Romans, countrymen, lend me your ears! I come to bury Caesar, not to praise him*. At the end of Mark Antony's anguished but carefully calculated speech, the crowd riots and civil war breaks out.

2. Make Fair Copies. Make clean, neat copies of the scene for each of the actors. If you use a photocopying machine, you can enlarge the print to make reading the script easier.

3. Cast Your Parts. If this is just a two-person scene, casting will be easy! Don't worry about gender. Remember, boys played female parts in Shakespeare's time.

4. Have a Read Through. Sit in a circle with your scripts in hand. Read through the scene and then talk about what is happening. To interpret the scene, ask and answer these four questions: Where does this scene take place? What is the scene about? When does it take place within the play? What is the purpose of the scene?

5. Analyze the Characters. In Shakespeare's day, there were no directors. The actors worked out all the details of the play among themselves. You can too! When considering how each part will be played, note the mood of the scene and each character's motivation. These things will determine your posture, gestures, and tone of voice. Pay attention to what your character does, says,

Home Again, Naturally Shakespeare Returns

bout 1611. William returns to Stratford-upon-Avon, settles down with his wife, and eventually dies—yet his work lives on to this day.

act 4, scene 1 At home by the Avon River.

William purchased New Place in 1597 for his wife and daughters. It had originally been built by Hugh Clopton a century earlier.

Full Circle, A Gentleman at New Place. After more than 20 years of a theater career in London, William finally returned to his boyhood town of Stratford-upon-Avon to enjoy his friends and family. He and his wife were grandparents now, but unfortunately, William's own mother had passed away the year William and Anne's granddaughter, Elizabeth, was born.

The lovely brick and timber house that he would now call home stood at the corner of Chapel Street and Chapel Lane. Located across the street from the familiar Guild Chapel and Grammar School, it was the second-largest house in town, boasting three stories, five gables, and ten fireplaces. Its frontage on Chapel Street was over 60 feet wide, and its depth was 70 feet or more along Chapel Lane. Surrounding his house were two gardens, two orchards, and two barns. Obviously, William was going to enjoy a leisurely, if short-lived, retirement.

Cares and Joys Abound. What did William do during this time? Certainly, just as he had kept watch over his holdings in Stratford while working in the capital city, now he tended to the investments he had made in London. Documents reveal that he returned to London in the last few years of his life, and in 1613, he even bought a gatehouse in the Blackfriars district—the home of the King's Mens' theater in winter—which he rented, but never lived in. At home, although he was not involved in politics as his father had been before him, he did take an interest in some of the town's affairs. For instance, William's name appears on a bill to parliament requesting that the national government lend funds for highway repair.

Surely, William, who had traveled to and from London for years, would have known about the condition of the roads.

In his personal life, he must have enjoyed the time he spent with his daughter, Judith, daughter Susanna and her husband, Dr. John Hall, and their daughter, Elizabeth. Elizabeth was a toddler when he returned to Stratford, an age by which children have acquired a vocabulary. So at least he was able to spend time playing and talking with her—time that he had missed with his own son and daughters.

A Garden of Verses. William used the language of flowers to paint pictures. Perhaps none is more beautiful than the verse he wrote in *A Midsummer Night's Dream*.

A Little Night Magic. Humble bees (bumblebees) buzz around honeyed-flowers with bewitching powers, birds on wing sing and flutter, and fairies abound with hardly a sound in the woods of *A Midsummer Night's Dream*. A fanciful story about the confusion and notion of love, it stars four couples: Hermia and Lysander, Titania and Oberon, Hippolyta and Theseus, and Helena and Demetrius.

Bottom, Titania, and fairies from *A Midsummer Night's Dream*

Here is a sample of the beautiful verse spoken of earlier:

Oberon [to Robin, his fairy assistant]:

> I know a bank where the wild thyme blows,
>
> Where oxlips and the nodding violet grows,
>
> Quite over-canopied with luscious woodbine,
>
> With sweet musk-roses, and with eglantine;
>
> There sleeps Titania sometime of the night,
>
> Lulled in these flowers with dances and delight;
>
> And there the snake throws her enameled skin,
>
> Weed wide enough to wrap a fairy in;
>
> And with the juice of this I'll streak her eyes,
>
> And make her full of hateful fantasies . . .

Oberon [casting a spell on Titania]:

> What thou seest when thou dost wake,
>
> Do it for thy true love-take;
>
> Love and languish for his sake.
>
> Be it ounce, or cat, or bear,
>
> Pard, or boar with bristled hair,
>
> In thy eye that shall appear
>
> When thou wak'st, it is thy dear:
>
> Wake when some vile thing is near.

While Titania is sleeping, Robin decides to have a little fun at her expense: Some men have gathered in the forest to rehearse a play that they will soon perform in honor of the marriage of Theseus and Hippolyta. Instead of letting Oberon's spell work as planned, Robin transforms the head of one of the men—Bottom—into that of a donkey. Upon seeing

Titania and Bottom

Definitions

Blows means bursts into flower. *Oxlips* are bright yellow flowers. *Woodbine* is honeysuckle. *Eglantine* is sweetbrier (a rose). *Throws her* means sheds its. *Weed* means garment. *Ounce* means lynx. *Cat* means lion or tiger. *Pard* means leopard.

him, his friends become frightened and run off. Only Bottom is unaware of the change in his appearance. To prove that he is not afraid, he sings a song, which awakens Titania. Guess what happens? She falls in love with Bottom! Upon hearing his voice, Titania says:

> I pray thee, gentle mortal, sing again.
> Mine ear is much enamored of thy note;
> So is mine eye enthralled to thy shape;

And thy fair virtue's force (perforce) doth move me
On the first view to say, to swear, I love thee.

Poor, *proud Titania*. While under the spell, she falls in love with Bottom.

When Titania awakens, she remembers the whole unsightly affair and says *My Oberon, what visions have I seen! Methought I was enamored of an ass*. It was a humiliating midsummer night!

Paint a Scene from A Midsummer Night's Dream

William Shakespeare's life and words have inspired many artists through the centuries. For example, Philip Calderon painted a colorful canvas of young Lord Hamlet playing piggyback with the court jester, Yorick, and a shimmering portrait of Juliet sitting by her window overlooking the garden. Henry Fuseli painted the scene of Hamlet talking to the ghost and a picture of Titania while under the influence of a magical spell in *A Midsummer Night's Dream*. And Charles Cattermole painted special moments from Shakespeare's life, some of which can be found in this book.

Calderon, Fuseli, and Cattermole—now, it's your turn to let Shakespeare inspire you!

Materials
* Copy of the play *A Midsummer Night's Dream*
* Any medium you desire—paint (oil, watercolor, tempera), chalk, pencil, ink, or charcoal
* Paper or any other surface of your choosing

Select a passage from the play. Perhaps you would like to draw a picture of the action taking place in the enchanted forest. Here is some dialogue that might inspire you: In Act 3, Scene 1, Titania has fallen in love with Bottom and is now instructing her tiny fairy attendants to take care of him:

Titania [to Bottom]:

> I'll give thee fairies to attend on thee;
> And they shall fetch thee jewels from the deep,
> And sing while thou on pressed flowers dost sleep.
> And I will purge thy mortal grossness so,
> That thou shalt like an aery spirit go.
> Peaseblossom! Cobweb! Moth! and Mustardseed!

Peaseblossom:

> Ready.

Cobweb:

> And I.

Moth:

> And I.

Mustardseed:

> And I.

All:

> Where shall we go?

Titania [to fairies]:

> Be kind and courteous to this gentleman,
> Hop in his walks and gambol in his eyes;
> Feed him with apricocks and dewberries,
> With purple grapes, green figs, and mulberries;
> The honey-bags steal from the humble-bees,
> And for night-tapers crop their waxen thighs,
> And light them at the fiery glow-worm's eyes,
> To have my love to bed and to arise;
> And pluck the wings from painted butterflies,
> To fan the moonbeams from his sleeping eyes.
> Nod to him, elves, and do him courtesies.

In the last scene of the play, Oberon and Titania instruct the fairies to bless the newly married couples sleeping in the Duke's house:

Oberon:

> Through the house give glimmering light

By the dead and drowsy fire,
Every elf and fairy sprite
Hop as light as bird from brier,
And this ditty, after me,
Sing, and dance it trippingly.

Titania:

> First, rehearse your song by rote,
> To each word a warbling note.
> Hand in hand, with fairy grace,
> Will we sing, and bless this place.

Oberon:

> Now, until the break of day,
> Through this house each fairy stray. . .

Now, select your medium and your surface and begin the act of creating your unique vision! Remember, this artwork doesn't have to be what's called "representational art"—it doesn't have to feature recognizable objects, people, or places—it can be what is known as abstract art. This allows you to create pictures of your feelings with color and movement. Or you can combine the two kinds of art. The choice is up to you!

act 4, scene 2 Meanwhile, there was excitement back in London.

Homeward Bound. When William returned home, he was still a relatively young and active man. Besides his business activities, it was here in Stratford that some historians believe he wrote his final plays, including *The Winter's Tale*, *The Tempest*, *Henry VIII*, and *Two Noble Kinsmen*. Many think that these last two plays were cowritten with John Fletcher, the man who succeeded him as chief playwright for the King's Men.

The Globe's Final Curtain? On June 29, 1613, when the King's Men had just begun their performance of *Henry VIII*, disaster struck. The directions in the fourth scene of the first act read: "drum and trumpet; chambers discharged." The chambers of the cannon were fired and the stuffing was shot from the cannon. Then, the hot packing material landed on the thatched roof and set it ablaze! Within two hours, the famous theater had burned to the ground.

Although one man's pants caught on fire and someone had to put it out with ale, miraculously, no one was killed or even badly hurt. But this fire did mark the end of an era because, as far as historians know, Shakespeare never wrote another play. Apparently, he spent his remaining years living his life in comfort surrounded by family and good friends.

The Globe: Part 2. Remarkably, William's plays were rescued from the fire. And, within one year, the Globe was rebuilt by the shareholders—this time with a tile roof. This theater would remain open for business on Bankside until 1642. Then, the English Civil War began, the theaters were closed, and finally, in 1644, the Globe was torn down.

Thankfully, however, theater returned 18 years later, in 1660, during the period known as the Restoration, which was when the exiled King Charles II returned to England. New plays were written for the new theaters being built—and actresses appeared on stage for the first time! Finally, audiences would hear and see a woman play Juliet, Beatrice, and Titania.

In 1970, there was another reason to celebrate when a fine American actor named Sam Wanamaker gathered a group of people to begin the process of rebuilding this theater near its original site. Completed in 1995, it was built in the same style as the original. When you visit England or watch a performance from the Globe on public television, you can experience theater as playgoers in Shakespeare's day did.

act 4, scene 3 William Shakespeare dies.

And Thereby Hangs a Tale. On April 23, 1616, William Shakespeare died. No one knows the circumstances surrounding his death, but we can presume that since his daughter Susanna's husband was a physician, he was well cared for.

A few months before he died, he met with his lawyer and asked him to draw up his last will and testament. The will was written on three sheets of parchment, and each page was signed. The last words of the will are "By me William Shakespeare." The first three words are written boldly, but by the time he got to writing his last name, it looks as though he might have been too weak to finish in his usual manner. His two signatures on the first two pages show, as well, that he may have lacked the strength to do this simple task.

It is in this document, which was discovered in 1747, that we get a glimpse of William Shakespeare the man.

Protective Father, Grandfather, and Brother. In 1607 and in 1613, William's brothers Edmund (who had followed William to London to become an actor) and Richard died. Now, of John and Mary Shakespeare's eight children, only Joan Shakespeare Hart remained.

Upon reading his will, one can see that William left behind a considerable estate. For his sister, he left £20 (20 pounds) and his clothes. Joan also was allowed to continue living in the western house on Henley Street for a small fee—12d (12 denarii), and her three sons, William, Michael, and Thomas, received £5 (five pounds) each. His granddaughter, Elizabeth Hall, received all the *silver plate* (silverware), except a bowl that was left to his daughter, Judith.

Soon after William signed his will in January 1616, his 31-year-old daughter Judith married Thomas Quiney (age 27). William had misgivings about this marriage, and he amended his will on March 25th to address these fatherly concerns. In this revision, he made sure that Judith and her children (if she had any) would be protected against her husband's claims. Thus, in addition to changing the language of his will to protect her interests, he left

Denarii

The "d" in 12d is the abbreviation for the Latin word *denarius*, a small silver coin of ancient Rome. One d was the equivalent of a penny. 12d = twelve pence

William Shakespeare's monument

her a silver-gilt bowl, money, and a promise for additional sums should she have living children three years from the date of the amended will.

Finally, to his daughter Susanna and her husband, John Hall, he left New Place and "all the rest of my goods, chattels, leases, plate, jewels, and household stuff whatsoever, after my debts and legacies paid and my funeral expenses discharged." These goods included the house in Blackfriars, the houses on Henley Street, and land.

Rings and Things. To his friends and neighbors, Hamnet Sadler, William Reynolds, Anthony Nash, and John Nash, and to chums and partners from the Lord Chamberlain's Men, William left money to buy memorial rings. In addition, he remembered Thomas Combe (nephew of the richest man in town) with his sword; his godson William Walker with 20s (20 shillings) in gold; and for the poor, he left £10 (10 pounds) with the almshouse, which was a large sum of money at that time.

Much Ado About Nothing? As a widowed person, his wife, Anne, would have been entitled to one-third of his estate and the right to live in her husband's home. But it is William's actual words that have intrigued scholars throughout the years, not what may or may not have been given to her under the law. Indeed, it is the bequest of the second-best bed that has puzzled historians for centuries. Some have written that the best bed may have simply been reserved for guests at New Place and so leaving her the second-best bed was not in the least insulting, as many have suggested. Others have speculated that the second-best bed had sentimental value for William and Anne, and thus his bequest was thoughtful and personal. Again, as he had in life, Shakespeare left us with another mystery to unravel.

Let It Be. Two days after his death, William was buried in the chancel of Holy Trinity Church. Because it was customary to dig up remains and bury them elsewhere, a warning was engraved on his tombstone, which may have been ordered by Shakespeare himself:

> Good friend for Jesus sake forbeare
> To digg the dust encloased heare:
> Bleste be the man that spares these stones,
> And curst be he that moves my bones.

And no one ever has.

One More Piece of Good Advice from Shakespeare

Grapple [your friends] unto [your] soul with hoops of steel.

In other words: Take good care of your friendships.

Bind Your Own Folio

In Shakespeare's day, a scribe rewrote William's work from foul papers, but a printer set type (prepared the printing press) from one of three (or perhaps all three) versions of the play: the foul papers, the scribe's fair copy, and the book of the play. This third version—the book of the play—was a fair copy with production notes made by a member of the company.

Sometimes, the text was incorrectly printed unintentionally, but other times this was done on purpose when the printer left out a word here and there to save money on paper. Unlike Shakespeare, though, you are the master of your folio!

Materials

❊ 3 or more pieces of lightweight paper 8½ by 11 inches

❊ Hole puncher

❊ 1 piece of watercolor-weight paper 9 by 12 inches

❊ Watercolors, marking pens, crayons, different-colored paper, or collage materials

❊ Pin

❊ Yarn, ribbon, or brass fasteners

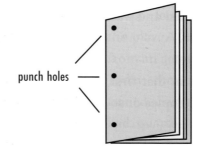

punch holes

Fold each of your three pieces of paper in half and form each crease with your hands. To get a really sharp crease, firmly press a ruler along each folded edge. The page should lie flat. Open one of the folded pieces of paper and place the second one inside so that the creases are touching. Now open that second folded piece of paper and place the third piece of paper inside so that its crease touches the second one's crease. Grouping sheets together in this fashion is a bookbinding term called "forming the signature." If you want a larger folio, continue making signatures (no more than 3 or 4 pieces of paper per signature).

Using the hole puncher, punch two to three holes in each signature, one signature at a time, using the first signature as a guide. Be sure to punch the holes at least ¼ inch away from the edge to avoid the risk of tearing.

Front and back covers: Fold the watercolor-weight piece of paper in half and decorate the top page, which will be the cover of your folio, with designs of your choosing. You may use watercolors, marking pens, crayons, different-colored paper, or collage material.

When your cover is complete, tuck the signature(s) inside, centering them on the cover.

Figure out exactly where the holes in the cover should go by carefully sticking a pin through each hole of the signature through to the cover. Then punch holes in the cover.

Thread yarn or ribbon through the holes to bind your book. Or, you can use brass fasteners.

Alternatively, you can create a larger book by using larger sheets of paper. If you want to make a scrapbook, use large sheets of heavyweight paper—the paper needs to be thick enough so that you can paste and attach things to it.

Now that you have a bound book, you are ready to begin filling it with art, poetry, mathematical equations, quotes, a story, and photos!

Recording the Past. Although documents exist that prove certain events in Shakespeare's life—baptismal records, a marriage bond, dedications to a patron for his long poems, a will—many pieces of the puzzle are missing. For instance, he didn't leave behind a diary with his words detailing his impressions of his family, his hometown, London, his theatrical experiences, marriage, or children. There are also no surviving notes on a playbill, drawings, or other mementos. Of course, we do have the most important part of his legacy—his work.

Start a Scrapbook

f Shakespeare had left a scrapbook like the one you are about to create, it would have been an added bonus.

Sometimes, we are so busy that we forget to stop and record those special moments and events in our lives. But it's a task worth considering. Think of it as a gift to yourself that you can enjoy right now and throughout your life and as a gift to future generations who might have fun learning about you and, consequently, their past.

Materials

* Large scrapbook
* Mementos: copy of birth certificate, newspaper clippings, photographs, pressed flowers, ticket stubs, badges, programs, cards, ribbons, award certificates, school records
* Adhesive-backed corners
* Pen
* Paper for writing captions (Captions can also be typed.)
* Scissors
* Double-sided tape

Optional decorative items: trims such as ribbon or lace, stickers, different-colored paper to use as background, and stencils

Optional: a tape recorder or video recorder is a nice addition to preserving important moments in your life!

Note: If you want to create an archival scrapbook, use archival paper, pens, corners, and tape. And never use regular transparent tape, rubber cement, or craft glue.

Exploring your past is the first step of the scrapbook process. This is the time for assembling the mementos you'd like to put in your scrapbook. Here are some examples of things for you to gather: a copy of your birth certificate; newspaper clippings; photographs; pressed flowers; ticket stubs from movies, plays, and airplane trips; badges; programs; cards; contest ribbons; award certificates, and school records (report cards, favorite essays). And don't forget to include your sonnet, coat of arms, and family tree!

Although the research and gathering phase of the scrapbook process may involve a bit of work, it is also the time when you will get to examine your past and make exciting discoveries.

Once you have your mementos in one place, the real fun begins, and you have at least three choices of how and when to arrange them:

1. Begin at the beginning with your birth and proceed from that special day forward.

2. Create a scrapbook of only holiday celebrations, or achievements, or trips. (If you are really ambitious, you can begin assembling many scrapbooks at once, each one for the different types of activities or events in your life.)

3. Or another way to begin is to start with today's events and journal entries and then go back into your past. That way, you are always up-to-date.

Whichever method you decide upon, here are a few suggestions to follow before you start attaching the mementos using the adhesive-backed corners:

Lay out the photos, articles, and other mementos on the page.

Leave room—white space—between the pieces so that the arrangement is pleasing to your eye.

You will also want to leave enough space between the pieces for a story or caption. Remember, you might know what significance a photo or badge has to you now, but in five or ten years, you may have forgotten many of the details. This is the time to get facts and stories down on paper!

Next, follow the instructions that come with the adhesive-backed corners. The reason these corners are best is that you can remove your items from the scrapbook without damaging them.

As for other items that cannot be held in place with corners, you can take pictures of them and place the originals in a memento box. Cassette tapes or videotapes could also be kept in the box. Or, if you don't mind permanently affixing mementos to your scrapbook page, use double-sided tape.

Finally, the use of color and three-dimensional items can give your scrapbook a special flair. For instance, you might want to decorate pages that contain photographs and mementos from a wedding with ribbons and lace. For sports pages, stickers with rackets, helmets, and baseballs, for example, would really add pizzazz. You can use different-colored papers to back your photos. And stencils can help add variety to any page.

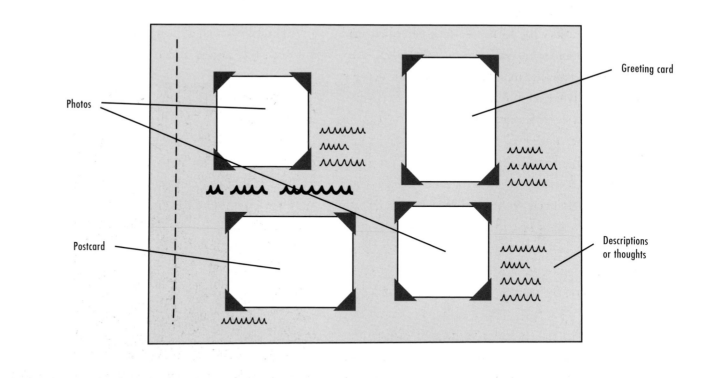

act 4, scene 4 Shakespeare lives on.

Inspiring Stuff. William Shakespeare continues to inspire us. Influenced by the arrangement and harmony of Shakespeare's words, composers have written operas and symphonies. For instance, Mendelssohn wrote "The Wedding March" for *A Midsummer Night's Dream*; Tchaikovsky composed a work called *Romeo and Juliet*; and Verdi wrote both the operatic version of *Othello* and a piece based on the character "Falstaff" from *The Merry Wives of Windsor*. Shakespeare, the man who would have learned to dance a jig as a young actor, has had his plays choreographed by Prokofiev in his 1940 ballet of *Romeo and Juliet* and by Jerome Robbins in the modern version of this classic tale called *West Side Story*.

Throughout the centuries, artists have interpreted scenes from Shakespeare's plays, creating dramatic tableaus in color and black and white. Irish artist Daniel Maclise painted the play-within-a-play scene from *Hamlet* and Sir John Millais gave us *Ophelia*.

When governments fall, we quote Shakespeare. When leaders die, we turn to his plays. In 1956, after antigovernment riots in Krakow, Poland, *Hamlet* was presented. In 1964, the year after President John F. Kennedy was killed, his brother Robert Kennedy spoke the lines from *Romeo and Juliet*:

> . . . and when [he] shall die,
> Take him and cut him out in little stars,
> And he will make the face of heaven so fine
> That all the world will be in love with night,
> And pay no worship to the garish sun.

The balcony scene from *West Side Story*, starring Richard Beymer and Natalie Wood

Lawrence Olivier acting in *Henry V*

Shakespeare, who advised *neither a borrower nor a lender be*, might be surprised to know that we borrow from him constantly and without apology. For example, the title of Aldous Huxley's most famous science fiction story, *Brave New World*, comes from a line from the play, *The Tempest*:

> O wonder!
> How many goodly creatures are there here!
> How beauteous mankind is! O brave new world
> That has such people in't!

Thanks to Shakespeare, we are never at a loss for words. At some point over the years, you are bound to use any one of his expressions such as *the be-all and the end-all*; *fair play*; *for goodness' sake*; *full circle*; *good riddance*; *knock, knock! who's there?*; *one fell swoop*; *what the dickens*; *what's done is done*; *wild-goose chase*; and *the world's mine oyster*.

Art, literature, music, politics, theater, and words, words, words!

Ben Jonson was right. Shakespeare "was not of an age, but for all time!"

Playbill for Shakespeare festival

YOUR PLACE in THIS WORLD of WONDERS

ere and Now. Shakespeare's plays had five acts. In this book, this final act is yours!

Such Stuff as Dreams Are Made On. What you have just read is a *remembrance of things past*. William Shakespeare's tale was retold because of the influence that his stories and varied words continue to have on language and the theater. We hope his achievements will inspire you to *strive mightily* to do whatever it is you love with imagination and passion.

And if you're ever unsure which road to take or which bridge to cross, just remember, *to thine own self be true*.

For *all the world's a stage* and we all play a vital part in it.

Places, everyone!

Glossary

after supper a light meal or dessert served after a big meal

anon soon

antique fables "tall" tales—tales with exaggerated, fantastical plots

bard poet

barnes children

belike probably

bubonic plague an epidemic disease. During the Elizabethan era, the plague was spread by rats and their fleas.

bum roll a padded roll worn around the hips, under a woman's skirt

canting when used in heraldry, this is a form of punning—a play upon words that has two meanings

crush a cup of wine have a drink

Elizabethan of or relating to the reign of Elizabeth I (1558–1603)

fair copy a manuscript with no markings or crossouts. This type of manuscript was typically prepared by a scribe and was easy for the actors to read.

farthingales stiffened hoops used in a woman's skirt

folio a sheet of paper that has been folded in half to make two leaves, or four pages

ford a shallow place in a stream or river where a person can cross

foul paper a writer's original manuscript marked with corrections and crossouts

foule stinkyng aire bad-smelling air

gambol skip

gauntlet the cuff for a glove

glover someone who makes gloves

good morrow good morning

groundlings theatergoers who would stand around the stage, on the ground. These were the inexpensive "seats" in the theater.

haply perhaps

hooping to shout with amazement and surprise

hornbook a wooden tablet that held a page of a school lesson

humble bees bumblebees

humours body fluids. Elizabethans believed that the human body contained four basic humours—blood, phlegm, choler, and black bile. The balance and amount of each of these fluids affected a person's personality and health.

hyperbole exaggeration

133

iambic pentameter a line of poetry that consists of 10 syllables, with each alternating syllable first unstressed then stressed

Jacobean of or relating to the reign of James VI of Scotland (1603–1625), also known as James I in England

Johannes fac totum a jack-of-all-trades

literati a Latin term for scholarly people

lost destroyed

metaphor comparing one thing to something else without using *like* or *as*

middle summer's spring the start of midsummer

midnight hags witches

motley multicolored

out of doubt surely

oxymoron a combination of words that have opposite meanings

personification giving an inanimate thing a life or personality

pied a variety of colors

pomander ball an aromatic ball made from a whole, dried fruit scented with spices. Elizabethans believed the pomander's scent would protect them from the plague.

remainder leftovers

ruff a large, round, pleated collar

simples medicinal herbs

skimble-skamble stuff nonsense

simile comparing one thing to something else by using *like* or *as*

soliloquy a speech in which the character speaks alone to the audience and reveals his innermost thought and feelings

sonnet a 14-line rhyming poem

straet the Old English word for ancient road

strolling much about to take the long way when walking

teetotum four-sided spinning top

tiring room a dressing room in the theater where costumes were stored

trippingly lightly, easily

trunk hose short, full pants reaching about halfway down the thigh

whittawer someone who transforms hides into white leather

workyday everyday

SHaKeSpeare's Plays

All's Well That Ends Well
Antony and Cleopatra
As You Like It
The Comedy of Errors
Coriolanus
Cymbeline
Hamlet
Henry IV, Part 1
Henry IV, Part 2
Henry V
Henry VI, Part 1
Henry VI, Part 2
Henry VI, Part 3
Henry VIII
Julius Caesar
King John
King Lear
Love's Labour's Lost
Macbeth

Measure for Measure
The Merchant of Venice
The Merry Wives of Windsor
A Midsummer Night's Dream
Much Ado About Nothing
Othello
Pericles
Richard II
Richard III
Romeo and Juliet
The Taming of the Shrew
The Tempest
Timon of Athens
Titus Andronicus
Troilus and Cressida
Twelfth Night
The Two Gentlemen of Verona
The Two Noble Kinsmen
The Winter's Tale

WEB SITES

Bird Source: Birding with a Purpose
http://birdsource.cornell.edu
A bird Web site created by the National Audubon Society and the Cornell Lab of Ornithology.

The Complete Works of William Shakespeare
http://www-tech.mit.edu/shakespeare/works.html
Sponsored by Massachusetts Institute of Technology, this site has the full text of all the plays and sonnets. The site also contains a dictionary of archaic terms.

Elizabethan England
http://www.springfield.k12.il.us/schools/springfield/eliz/elizabethanengland.html
Created by seniors at Springfield High School, this site is an introduction to the Elizabethan period of English history and literature. All articles were written by students. Contains pictures of the Tower of London.

Folger Library
http://www.folger.edu
This research library in Washington, D.C., is home to the largest collection of Shakespearean printed material in the world.

Legends: Swashbucklers and Fops
http://www.legends.dm.net/swash/rapier.html
A metasite for primary resources on period sword fighting.

Merriam-Webster's Word Central for Kids
http://www.wordcentral.com
Features a word of the day and an on-line student dictionary.

Mr. William Shakespeare and the Internet
http://daphne.palomar.edu/shakespeare
A metasite with links to other Shakespeare sites. Contains an excellent timeline, which is a great introduction to the bard's life.

The Shakespeare Oxford Society Page
http://www.shakespeare-oxford.com
This site debates the authorship of Shakespeare's plays.

Renaissance Image Gallery
http://www.english.upenn.edu/~bushnell/english-101/gallery.html
Created by Professor Rebecca Bushnell for her University of Pennsylvania English class, this Web site features a collection of over two dozen images from the Renaissance period.

Renaissance, the Elizabethan World
  http://www.renaissance.dm.net
  Brief historical synopses about common, everyday Elizabethan-era life. Topics include money and coinage, games, food, and education and schooling.
Shakespeare Birthplace Trust
  http://www.shakespeare.org.uk
  Visit Shakespeare's hometown in Stratford-upon-Avon.

Shakespeare's Globe
  http://www.shakespeares-globe.org
  Learn about the original Globe and newly reconstructed Globe. Includes great close-up photos of the stage and play performances.

BIBLIOGRAPHY

Adorjan, Carol, and Uri Rasovsky. *WKID: Easy Radio Plays*. Niles, Illinois: Albert Whitman & Company, 1988.

Arnold, Caroline. *Juggle*. Boston, Massachusetts: Ticner and Fields, 1988.

Barroll, Leeds. *Politics, Plague, and Shakespeare's Theater*. Ithaca, NY, and London: Cornell University Press, 1991.

Beebe, Ruth Anne. *Sallets, Humbles, and Shrewsbery Cakes: A Collection of Elizabethan Recipes*. Boston, Massachusetts: David R. Godine, 1976.

Besmehn, Bobby. *Juggling Step-by-Step*. New York: Sterling Publishing Company, 1995.

Boyce, Charles. *Shakespeare A to Z*. New York: A Roundtable Press Book/Delta Trade Paperbacks, 1990.

Brown, Ivor. *How Shakespeare Spent the Day*. New York: Hill and Wang, 1963.

Burgess, Anthony. *Shakespeare*. New York: Alfred A. Knopf, 1970.

Cassidy, John, and B. C. Rimbeaux. *Juggling for the Complete Klutz*. Palo Alto, California: Klutz, 1994.

Claybourne, Anna, and Rebecca Treays. *The World of Shakespeare*. London: Usborne Publishing, Ltd., 1996.

Davis, Justin Michael. *The England of William Shakespeare*. New York: EP Dutton, 1987.

Durant, David N. *Where Queen Elizabeth Slept and What the Butler Saw*. New York: St. Martin's Press, 1996.

Encyclopaedia Britannica. Chicago: William Benton, 1969.

Epstein, Norrie. *Friendly Shakespeare*. New York: Penguin Books, 1993.

Evans, G. Blakemore, et al. *The Riverside Shakespeare 2nd Ed*. New York: Houghton Mifflin Company, 1997.

Finnigan, Dave. *The Complete Juggler*. New York: Vintage Books, 1987.

Fraser, Russell. *Young Shakespeare*. New York: Columbia University Press, 1988.

Gifford, Clive. *The Usborne Book of Juggling*. London: Usborne Publishing, 1995.

Grout, Donald Jay. *A History of Western Music*. New York: WW Norton & Co., Inc., 1960.

Gurr, Andrew. *William Shakespeare: The Extraordinary Life of the Most Successful Writer of All Time*. New York: HarperPerennial, 1995.

Gurr, Andrew, and John Orrell. *Rebuilding Shakespeare's Globe*. New York: Routledge Theater Arts Book, 1989.

Halliday, F. E. *Shakespeare*. New York: Thames and Hudson, Inc., 1956.

Halliday, F. E. *Shakespeare in His Age*. New York: Thomas Yoseloff, 1964.

Hill, Wayne F., and Cynthia J. Ottchen. *Shakespeare's Insults*. New York: Crown Trade Paperbacks, 1991.

Hodges, C. Walter. *Shakespeare and the Players*. New York: Coward-McCann, 1963.

Kerr, Jessica. *Shakespeare's Flowers*. New York: HarperCollins Publishers, 1969.

Kite, L. Patricia. *Gardening Wizardry for Kids*. Hauppauge, New York: Barron's Educational Series, Inc., 1995.

Kott, Jan. *Shakespeare Our Contemporary*. Garden City, New York: Doubleday and Company, 1974.

Laroque, Francois. *The Age of Shakespeare*. New York: Harry N. Abrams, 1993.

Levi, Peter. *The Life and Times of William Shakespeare*. New York: Henry Holt and Company, 1988.

Macrone, Michael. *Brush Up Your Shakespeare*. New York: HarperPerennial, 1990.

Marder, Louis. *Speak the Speech: The Shakespeare Quotation Book*. New York: HarperPerennial, 1994.

McDonald, Russ. *The Bedford Companion to Shakespeare: An Introduction with Documents*. Boston: Bedford Books, 1996.

McMurtry, Jo. *Understanding Shakespeare's England: A Companion for the American Reader*. Hamden, Connecticut: Archon Books, 1989.

McQuain, Jeffrey, and Stanley Malless. *Coined by Shakespeare*. Springfield, Massachusetts: Merriam-Webster, Inc., 1998.

Miner, Margaret, and Hugh Rawson. *A Dictionary of Quotations from Shakespeare*. New York: Meridian, 1992.

Morgan, Professor Kenneth O., et al. *The Young Oxford History of Britain and Ireland*. New York: Oxford University Press, 1996.

Morrill, John. *The Oxford Illustrated History of Tudor and Stuart Britain*. New York: Oxford University Press, 1996.

Onions, C. T., and Robert D. Eagleson, eds. *A Shakespeare Glossary*. New York: Oxford University Press Inc., 1986.

Parrott, Thomas Marc. *Shakespeare, Twenty-Three Plays and Sonnets*. New York: Charles Scribner's Sons, 1938.

Potter, Tony, Ed. *The Usborn Book of London*. England: Usborne Publishing, Ltd., 1987.

Rowland-Warne, L., et al. *Costume*. New York: Alfred A. Knopf, 1992.

Rowse, A. L. *William Shakespeare, A Biography*. New York: Harper and Row, Publishers, 1963.

Schmidt, Alexander. *Shakespeare Lexicon and Quotation Dictionary*. New York: Dover Publications Inc., 1971.

Schoenbaum, S. *William Shakespeare, A Compact Documentary Life*. New York: Oxford University Press, 1987.

Singman, Jeffrey L. *Daily Life in Elizabethan England*. Connecticut: Greenwood Press, 1995.

Stanley, Diane, and Peter Vennema. *Bard of Avon*. New York: Morrow Junior Books, 1992.

Stokes, Donald and Lillian. *Bird Gardening Book*. Boston: Little Brown & Company, 1998.

The Compact Edition of the Oxford English Dictionary. Oxford, England: Oxford University Press, 1971.

Whalen, Richard F. *Shakespeare—Who Was He?* Westport, Connecticut: Praeger Press, 1994.

Wilson, Ian. *Shakespeare the Evidence*. New York: St. Martin's Press, 1993.

Wright, Louis B. *Shakespeare's England*. New York: Harper and Row, 1964.

PHOTO CREDITS

viii Portrait of Shakespeare. Courtesy of the Library of Congress.

CHAPTER 1
2 Plan of Stratford-Upon-Avon. (Samuel Winter's map.) Courtesy of the Records Office, Shakespeare Birthplace Trust, Stratford-Upon-Avon.

3 Schematic map of Henley Street during Shakespeare's time, Pat Hughes. Courtesy of the Records Office, Shakespeare Birthplace Trust, Stratford-Upon-Avon.

4 Shakespeare's birthplace on Henley Street. Courtesy of the Records Office, Shakespeare Birthplace Trust, Stratford-Upon-Avon.

5 Holy Trinity Church. Courtesy of the Records Office, Shakespeare Birthplace Trust, Stratford-Upon-Avon.

5 Baptism record of William Shakespeare. Courtesy of the Records Office, Shakespeare Birthplace Trust, Stratford-Upon-Avon.

6 Living room, Shakespeare's birthplace. Courtesy of the Records Office, Shakespeare Birthplace Trust, Stratford-Upon-Avon.

14 Charles Cattermole. *Scenes from Shakespeare's Life: Shakespeare Meets the Strolling Players*. Courtesy of the University of Warwick History of Art Photograph Collection.

15 Payment to the players, 1569. Courtesy of the Records Office, Shakespeare Birthplace Trust, Stratford-Upon-Avon.

16 Robert Dudley, Earl of Leicester. Courtesy of the National Portrait Gallery, London.

22 Tudor desk. Courtesy of the Records Office, Shakespeare Birthplace Trust, Stratford-Upon-Avon.

23 King Edward VI School. Courtesy of the Records Office, Shakespeare Birthplace Trust, Stratford-Upon-Avon.

72 Inn yard. Courtesy of the Library of Congress.

73 Burial record of Hamnet Shakespeare. Courtesy of the Records Office, Shakespeare Birthplace Trust, Stratford-Upon-Avon.

74 Eighteenth-century watercolor of The Globe. Courtesy of the British Museum.

75 Greenwich Palace. Courtesy of the Ashmolean Museum.

76 The Shakespeare coat of arms. Courtesy of the Records Office, Shakespeare Birthplace Trust, Stratford-Upon-Avon.

79 The theaters in London. Courtesy of the Library of Congress.

80 Cross section of the Globe theater from Shakespeare's second Globe by C. Walter Hodges (1973), reprinted by permission of Oxford University Press.

81 Reconstruction drawing of The Globe stage. Courtesy of the Library of Congress.

89 Robert Devereux, 2nd Earl of Essex. Courtesy of the National Portrait Gallery, London.

90 Charles Cattermole, *Scenes from Shakespeare's Life: Shakespeare Acting Before Queen Elizabeth*. Courtesy of the University of Warwick History of Art Photograph Collection.

93 John Henry Fuseli, *The Witches*. Courtesy of the University of Warwick History of Art Photograph Collection.

CHAPTER 4
108 New Place. Courtesy of the Library of Congress.

110, 111 Film stills from *Midsummer Night's Dream* (1935). Courtesy of Photofest.

118 Shakespeare's monument. Courtesy of the Records Office, Shakespeare Birthplace Trust, Stratford-Upon-Avon.

120 Title page for *First Folio*. Courtesy of the Records Office, Shakespeare Birthplace Trust, Stratford-Upon-Avon.

121 Droushout portrait, *First Folio*. Courtesy of the Records Office, Shakespeare Birthplace Trust, Stratford-Upon-Avon.

127 Film still from *West Side Story* (1962). Courtesy of Photofest.

128 Film still from *Henry V* (1945). Courtesy of Photofest.

129 Playbill for Shakespeare festival. Courtesy of the Library of Congress.

acknowledgments

Margie Blumberg

I would like to acknowledge the important people in my life who stood beside me throughout this journey and to thank some new friends who graciously gave of themselves for the betterment of this book.

First, I want to thank my parents for instilling a passion for learning and a love of words and theater. Mom, you're a rock, and I will love and rely on you always. And Dad, your editing was superb. And because you did it with patience and joy, even when you had so many other things on your plate, I will be forever grateful.

I also want to thank my wonderful boyfriend for his constant encouragement, kind heart . . . and hot soup—and for letting me read draft after draft to him! Love and thanks also to my sister for lending an ear in times of frustration and joy; my brother for his never-ending love and support; and my nephews, for their humor, which served as a great escape. Also, special thanks to my older nephew for drawing that fantastic pomander ball! Gratitude also to my dearest companions for keeping in touch throughout this process. Special valentines must go to Debby Feld Skobel, Laura Shack, and Fran Berger Kahn. Other friends and relatives I'd like to thank are Joe Zalis, Karen Brick, Lillibeth Burgos, Lori Lazaroff, Chris Kahn, Rosario de la Barra, Bernadette Estella, April Mott, Craig Wolf, Jo McCarty, Jane Roemer, Sherry Kinland Kaswell, Janet Weissman, Paul Frieden, Sylvia Berkow, Elly Idas, Wendy Berkow, Joe Berk, Mayumi and Roy Gottlieb, and Edie and Marvin Catler. I love you all! A special note of appreciation must go to John Thompson for keeping the faith through three presidencies. And finally, to my nana, Anna Zalis, and Terry Motak, who are always in my heart.

Thanks also to two of my favorite English teachers, Mr. Robertshaw and Mr. Barrett, for their infectious enthusiasm.

Much gratitude must go to Cynthia Sherry for shepherding this book through to acceptance, and Rita Baladad, whose care and patience and thoughtful editing were so instrumental.

Many thanks to Tom Hentoff of Williams & Connoly for his wisdom and friendship.

When writing a biography that includes activities, one must rely not only on books but also on the expertise of practitioners. So, when books were not enough . . .

Thanks to Herb Zalis, bird-watcher extraordinaire, for his patience and erudition. Gratitude also to Carl Van Doren (Wild Bird Center, Potomac, Maryland) for sharing his expertise on creating a bird habitat and those wonderful recipes for our "fine feathered friends"; Timm Cross (Johnson's Flower Center, Kensington, Maryland) and Michael Zalis for explaining the story of plants; Barry Wood, magician (Washington, D.C.), for magically appearing just in time to teach me his approach to juggling; Sara Glik, professional photographer and teacher (Baltimore, Maryland), for explaining the fine art of bookmaking and for her creativity for the folio, bookbinding, and goblet activities; Julia Loeb (Rockville, Maryland) for sharing her knowledge of scrapbooks; Brad Waller, workshop leader and guest curator at the Folger Library and professor of stage combat at Catholic University, George Mason University, and The Shakespeare Theatre, for his expert advice on designing a safe sword and sword fight; and Mr. Waller's assistants, Elizabeth Williams and Kathryn Barnhardt, for demonstrating the art of sword fighting.

For cheerfulness and professionalism in the face of a tight deadline, recognition must go to editorial consultant Keira L. Roberts, Production Editor of the Shakespeare Quarterly, for shining through; Edward Gero, Shakespearean actor and professor at George Mason University, for giving the manuscript a careful reading and for introducing me to Brad Waller; and Lisa Hartjens of Imagefinders (Washington, D.C.), for her enthusiasm for this project and stick-to-it-iveness while seeking all those permissions for the pictures.

Others I would like to thank are Richard Kuhta, Librarian, Folger Library, for sending that amazing bibliography; Patricia McFarland of Stratford-upon-Avon for sharing those inspirational pictures of *Mr. Quatremain's Stratford*; Ann Donnelly, Museums Curator of The Shakespeare Birthplace Trust; Willis and Carter Van Devanter of the Thankful Chase, Poolesville, Maryland, for allowing me to peruse and take notes from their unique books on Renaissance food; and the employees of Rockville Printing and Graphics (Rockville, Maryland), and Imatek (Washington, D.C.), for their great work and good cheer. It was truly a pleasure working with all of them!

For motivation and phrasing that can't be beat—other than that provided by William Shakespeare himself, of course—I am most grateful to these talented composer/lyricist teams and interpreters of great music: Jerry Leiber and Mike Stoller, Richard Rodgers and Oscar Hammerstein II, Alan Jay Lerner and Frederick Loewe, Jerry Herman, Cole Porter, Jimmy Van Heusen and Sammy Cahn, Sheldon

Harnick and Jerry Bock, Johnny Mercer and Howard Arlen, Stephen Sondheim, Frank Sinatra, Sammy Davis, Jr., Tommy Steele, and the Beatles. They all gave me "high hopes!"

Last, but not least, thanks to Mr. William Shakespeare, a man whose life, for a brief moment, collided with mine. It was an exhilarating ride!

Colleen Aagesen

A heartfelt thanks to the following Nebraskans and Washingtonians: Marlene Bernstein and Dan Daly for giving their Shakespeare expertise to the manuscript, Kevin Barratt for the stage dueling and battling knowledge he shared with me, Mike Cowles for his assistance in a stage duel activity, my brother Neil Harper for the drawings he prepared for the illustrators, my sister Marla Krug for the theater background she brought to the manuscript, my brother Mark Harper for his help in the juggling activity, Evan Thompson for her computer assistance, Donna Eipperle for her costuming guidance, Joan Prenosil for her advice on madrigals, Kevin Krug for his research assistance, Ellen Plath for her help on the sonnet activity, and Sue Morris for her gardening and goblet ideas. Along with my co-author, I thank Rita Baladad, project editor; Cynthia Sherry, senior editor; and Linda Matthews, publisher of Chicago Review Press. We collectively thank the Folger Library, Patricia McFarland of Stratford-upon-Avon, and Lisa Hartjens of Imagefinders. Finally, I would like to thank my parents, Royce and Charlotte Harper, for their unfailing support; my husband, Bert, for his patience; my mother-in-law, Lilleba Aagesen, for her encouragement; my children—Kathryn, Carl, and Eric—for so willingly giving me their reactions; my students through the years who responded to a hands-on approach; and my sister, Ivy Harper, who helped conceive this wonderful project.